T0128960

Pray Through It!

Daughters of Christ

A spiritual guide for a teenage girl during her adolescent years

Bianca A. Douglas

authorHOUSE®

AuthorHouse™
1663 Liberty Drive
Bloomington, IN 47403
www.authorhouse.com
Phone: 833-262-8899

Published by AuthorHouse 06/24/2021

ISBN: 978-1-6655-1714-0 (sc)
ISBN: 978-1-6655-1713-3 (e)

Library of Congress Control Number: 2021903299

Print information available on the last page.

CONTENTS

High School Blues

Random Knowledge

DEDICATION

First, I would like to acknowledge My Lord and Savior Jesus Christ for placing the idea on my heart to write this book, Thank you Father. Second, I would like to dedicate this book to my three girls. My daughters Mia (19 yrs. old) who first stole my heart when I was 16 yrs. old. Mia, you had to go through those rough times with me as I received the wisdom that I am sharing with you in this book. I thank you boo, for being patient with me as I matured into my womanhood and as I found my way through life. Jaila (9 yrs. old), thank you boo for being such a sweetheart and loving me regardless of my short comings and finally my granddaughter, McKenzi (9 months), who is just the sweetest baby anyone could ask for. I mean she literally wakes up smiling and clapping her hands. She is such a blessing, thank you, Mia.

When the idea was first placed on my heart to write this book, I was hesitant, and I was scared. With the negative thoughts going through my mind of not knowing enough to be titled an author, I wasn't anyone "famous" for anyone to listen to and I did not have enough to write. All I knew was I trust the Lord and I love to write so He said make it happen, now look at this. The Lord told me to write down the life lessons that I have learned over the years, so that my daughters would benefit from knowing.

This was in the beginning of my rebuilding phase of a relationship with my biological father. He wasn't a part of my life as I grew up and all I really knew about him was that he had Spinal Cerebellar Ataxia-3. During the years when I reached back out to him. With the need for a man to help guide me, through the times of dating boys (who claimed to be men), it was too late. It was hard to understand him due to the nature of the disease,

SCA-3 it could eventually impair your speech, mobility, swallowing and your vision. In worse cases such as his it had weakened his muscles. Sad to say I had waited too long to be able to communicate with him effectively. Knowing his condition was genetic, and that I have a 50/50 chance of developing this disease. Spinal Cerebellar Ataxia-3 then, became a fear of mine in my earlier years, a fear that I would develop it and end up like my father. God used that fear and pushed me into my purpose. I thought, the purpose of writing these mental notes down was to be a guide to navigate my own daughters through the hard times they will face in life. If it came a point in time where I was not able to tell them myself but God, wanted me to provide all of his children with this information. Today, I understand that this is just the beginning of my journey.

As time went on, I began thinking of all the information I would have benefited from if someone would have told me sooner in life. How many of y'all already know your plans are minor compared to Gods plans for your life? As time went on it became clear to me that the ways of the world were changing and the young ladies of today need more guidance than ever before. The Lord has showed me that he allowed me to go through all the hurt, pain, and setbacks to be a living example that He is the Author of our stories and He has the final say. He placed the mission on my heart to help prepare all his daughters who may also become bruised or broken by the events of life or just need a little guidance in the right direction. Also, to show you that whatever you are facing is not the end, pray through it, the Lord will provide you the strength to endure and peace to forgive those who may hurt you. By seeking the Lord, reading his promises and through him, you will be able to overcome everything you are faced with. If I can do it, you can also.

God is our Father and the only man to depend on. One of his promises is He will never leave you or forsake (abandon) you. When you start to believe this everything, you encounter will become bearable. Just knowing He is with you while you are going through your situation is enough to help you through it. Thank you, Father for loving me despite of my repeated bad choices. Thank you for trusting me to write this book for your daughters. My prayer is this will make an impact on all of you who may read it and you not just store this knowledge but begin to apply it to your life. In Jesus Holy name, Amen.

INTRODUCTION

This book is the result of years of doing the wrong things but wanting the right things to happen. When you decide to walk with Christ it requires you to willingly want to change. Change begins with your thinking. Whatever you think determines how you act. Change is not an overnight process or even a year process it is a continual decision. It took a long time for me to fully understand that this life is not my own; I have a creator, I was created for a purpose, and until I realized my purpose was to be like Christ-walking in his image and likeness and serving his people while here on earth, I was lost. The thought that I was in control of my destiny and things should go as I planned. Boy, was I wrong!! Who better to tell you your purpose than the one who created you?

Ask the Lord: what is my purpose? Patiently wait for the answer. Once he makes it clear to you, begin to walk towards your purpose, and things will start to make sense. Now, I am not saying you must be perfect because no one is perfect but God, but the drive to be obedient to the word is all the Lord is requesting. I prayed and asked God for understanding. Then the Lord began showing me about myself, he gave me wisdom, and made it clear that I was not applying my knowledge to what I was supposed to do. This goes to show just because you know better does not always mean you will do better. Being hardheaded did not help and took a whole lot longer to finally commit to the decision to change. Once you understand the way the Lord has designed you to serve his people, do it, and do it with a cheerful heart. We all must accept that we are all flesh of man or woman. Trust and believe we will all make mistakes even after we decide to change our ways and decide to be in the army of the Lord, attempting to walk in righteousness. God already knew we would sin and that is why he sent his son to show mankind the righteous way. Then allowed his son, Jesus to die for our sins so we would not have to.

He died knowing we all will fall short of glory but, no one is exempt from God's Grace and Mercy. If you keep attempting to chase after the Lord, he will see your heart and give you grace. As you read this book, I am going to share with you some of the things that I feel if I would have known earlier, would have helped guide me through my teenage years - the years when I thought I knew it all. I really thought I was making good choices, based on what I wanted. Now, I understand my life is not about me. I am here for a greater purpose and God has a calling over my life, just as well as He does yours.

Once you decide to run towards Christ, you will have many obstacles to overcome. Your number one enemy is after you now. The devil is real, and he is your enemy, boo. He has no good intentions for you at all and he takes NO days off. All the bad things that happen in life, evolve from him. He will try to tempt you by exposing your weaknesses to throw you off the path of righteousness. He is influential. The enemy comes only to steal, kill, and destroy all your hopes and dreams. The enemy is a fallen angel, who chose bad over good and now that you are choosing to run with Christ, and not the devil, he does not like that. So, he will begin to strategically place every obstacle in the form of a distraction, set back, heart ache, abuse, death of loved ones, molestation, and physical pain, whatever is needed your way to deter you and make you feel as though this decision was the wrong one. Why, because he does not want you to turn away from sin. Good thing to know is God uses everything for the good of those who love him. The good, the bad, the pain, and the setbacks you experience will all be used for your glory. Nothing that is formed against you shall prosper. Keep your faith!! You only lose if you quit. Allow yourself to grow closer in Christ during this time in your life and as you read this book. I pray that this book helps you do just that.

Incorporated is a small prayer after each chapter because I was told being a Christian without prayer is like being alive without breathing – Martin Luther. I was also told a proverb a day will keep the demons away. So, enjoy these nuggets. Let me warn you, I may repeat myself at times throughout the book but just as I tell my kids, "just nod and say ok." Repetition is key to remembering and confirmation comes in the form of 2's & 3's. Remember, baby girl, Jesus Loves you.

Let us begin...

Love God First

CHAPTER 1

Build a relationship with your Lord and Savior Jesus Christ

W hen building a healthy relationship with anyone it is a voluntary and gradual process. It takes consistency and free will. The Lord wants a relationship with you because he is your father, but he will not force a relationship upon you. He wants you to come to him voluntarily. To believe the words stated in the Bible, the words of God, you must know who God is. God is your father in Heaven. Let me give you a little background to how I understand who God is, but again you really need to read the bible to get a better understanding or attend a teaching church like mine, shout out to Grace Church, www. Gracechurchva.org. The Lord and savior Jesus Christ consist of the father, (God), the son, (Jesus), and the Holy Spirit (Gods continual presence here on earth). This is called the trinity. When you give your life to Christ you are saying, yes Lord, I will trust you, I will be obedient to your word, I will not try to do it on my own anymore but allow you to direct my steps. You will then be filled with the Holy Spirit, so when someone says God is always with you this is what they mean. God is all power, He is amazing, He is wonderful, He is your protector, He is your way maker, miracle worker, light in the darkness, He knows the beginning and the end of everything that happens. He is your creator, and He always has your best interest in the forefront. He will never lead you astray. God is an awesome

God and until you experience the Holy Spirit for yourself you will not understand what I am talking about. Throughout this book I will switch back and forth between using Jesus, Lord and God I am speaking about the same almighty King.

Once you build your relationship with the Lord, you will see that all you need is Him. He wants to show you the kind of love that he has for you, you cannot get anywhere else. He wants you to know that with Him all things are possible. There was a whole book written for the sole purpose of expressing his promises to you. He knows your every need before you do, He knows the desires of your heart, He knows your weaknesses and your strengths. He knows it all. There is nothing you can hide from the almighty King. Your father is a King so that automatically makes you a Princess, so all He wants is for you to live up to that standard, boo. You are worth so much and once you realize that life will begin to make sense. He created you for a purpose and without hearing from your creator you will not know your purpose. Living without knowing your purpose is kind of like running around like a chicken with your head cut off - running around until you get tired and eventually die. So, this is a decision that is strictly up to you. You can try it on your own but, over time you will see that your worst day with Jesus is better than your best day without Him. Then and only then you will begin to believe wholeheartedly that Jesus is the way, the truth, and the light in your darkest moments.

It took me years to get to the point where I am so grateful for whatever happens in my life. I thank the Lord multiple times a day, for the good and the bad, why because I know Gods got me. Believing his word and allowing my steps to be directed by his will. I finally arrived at the point where I was tired of living in sin, or should I say the way I wanted. All God is wanting, is for you to be obedient to his word and he will give you all your heart's desires. He will satisfy all your needs. Do not read this and think I am trying to shame you in any way. Lord knows I am far from perfect, but I do try to walk right every day. I am a work in progress. I may stumble, then repent. This is a forever walk. It is a process, that no one can put a time frame on but just try to keep your heart pure and free of malice.

Prayer is a big part of building your relationship. Prayer is simply communicating with God about your thoughts. Although he knows your thoughts before speaking them, prayer is making it verbally known that you need help, and you are asking for help from your father. I did not always pray or listen to gospel music. I was once upon a time not a Christian. Oh, do not get it twisted, I still have moments when I may doubt something or do not always go to the Lord first, did I mention I am still a work in progress? Your relationship with the lord is unique, He knows how He must speak to you. It takes time to build up to knowing when the Lord is speaking to you. After 35 years and finally realizing that there is no one greater, stronger, or more powerful than my father in Heaven, I had to submit to the Christian walk. Patience is understanding that everyone comes to Christ on their own timing. Do not judge the next person because Christ loves us all, although we all have sinned.

Get into healthy habits, I tell my daughters and my stepson to thank the lord every morning for waking them up, pray you have a blessed day. Even if that is all you do every day. Acknowledge the Lord first before your feet hit the floor as soon as your eyes open. This is an example of putting God first. Thank the Lord throughout the day because He did not have to wake up or allow your alarm to go off or a bed for you to wake up in, or even allow your legs to work so you could walk. Be grateful for all things that you have because some people are not as fortunate to be able to do a lot of the things you are able to do. Even the little things that we overlook such as talking, brushing your teeth, showering yourself & using the bathroom on your own. In everything, give thanks. When the Lord begins to speak, listen. It will be those small still voices that you brush off at times, they are needed to help guide your steps. If you ignore them, they will become silent. This is a part of trust when building your relationship with the Lord.

My daughter, Jaila, must read for 20 mins a day for school, so I tell her to read the bible. She also tries to remember scripture and pray nightly. These habits are a part of building up her relationship with the Lord. I explain to her that whenever she may feel scared, sad, hurt, alone or doubtful just speak to the lord and he will hear your heart cries. You do not have to sound like a pastor or a seasoned church member when you talk to God. He will meet you where you are. Talk to Him as if he is your friend. Tell Him what is on your heart as if He does not already know. *"Humble yourselves in the presence of the Lord, and he will exalt you"*. (New American Standard Bible, James 4:10). Start off by reciting some of His promises to you, the familiar ones, can be found in the book of Psalms in the Bible. Daily communication with the Lord is the goal of building a healthy relationship. This is by far the most important relationship for anyone to have. He wants to be your everything! As he should be. Again, I urge you to read the Bible for yourself. It is complex depending on the version you choose but, as you read, it will begin to make sense. You can ask the Lord for anything especially, understanding of his word to you.

The dictionary and other search engines are your friend when you hit a word you do not understand, look it up. So, it can be made clear to you. When reading the Bible, you must read it a few times before you really understand and apply it to your life. It is the book of life. A guide on how to live life the right way. Literally, the Bible is our instruction manual. As you continue to encounter the events in life the Bible will begin to make more sense.

Prayer: Lord Thank you for accepting me as I am. Your word says even though I am a sinner you died for me. Thank you, Lord, for Jesus. I come to you with open arms to receive your everlasting, unconditional, reckless love. Help me to understand your word as I begin my walk with you. Please direct my steps, Lord. I give you all the Praise and Honor in Jesus name, Amen.

New International Version, Proverbs 1

Purpose and Theme
1 The proverbs of Solomon son of David, king of Israel:
2
for gaining wisdom and instruction;
    for understanding words of insight;

3
for receiving instruction in prudent behavior,
   doing what is right and just and fair;
4
for giving prudence to those who are simple,[a]
   knowledge and discretion to the young—
5
let the wise listen and add to their learning,
   and let the discerning get guidance—
6
for understanding proverbs and parables,
   the sayings and riddles of the wise.[b]
7
The fear of the Lord is the beginning of knowledge,
   but fools[c] despise wisdom and instruction.
Prologue: Exhortations to Embrace Wisdom
Warning Against the Invitation of Sinful Men
8
Listen, my son, to your father's instruction
   and do not forsake your mother's teaching.
9
They are a garland to grace your head
   and a chain to adorn your neck.
10
My son, if sinful men entice you,
   do not give in to them.
11
If they say, "Come along with us;
   let's lie in wait for innocent blood,
   let's ambush some harmless soul;
12
let's swallow them alive, like the grave,
   and whole, like those who go down to the pit;
13
we will get all sorts of valuable things
   and fill our houses with plunder;

14
cast lots with us;
    we will all share the loot"—
15
my son, do not go along with them,
    do not set foot on their paths;
16
for their feet rush into evil,
    they are swift to shed blood.
17
How useless to spread a net
    where every bird can see it!
18
These men lie in wait for their own blood;
    they ambush only themselves!
19
Such are the paths of all who go after ill-gotten gain;
    it takes away the life of those who get it.
Wisdom's Rebuke
20
Out in the open wisdom calls aloud,
    she raises her voice in the public square;
21
on top of the wall[d] she cries out,
    at the city gate she makes her speech:
22
"How long will you who are simple love your simple ways?
    How long will mockers delight in mockery
    and fools hate knowledge?
23
Repent at my rebuke!
    Then I will pour out my thoughts to you,
    I will make known to you my teachings.
24
But since you refuse to listen when I call
    and no one pays attention when I stretch out my hand,

25

since you disregard all my advice
  and do not accept my rebuke,

26

I in turn will laugh when disaster strikes you;
  I will mock when calamity overtakes you—

27

when calamity overtakes you like a storm,
  when disaster sweeps over you like a whirlwind,
  when distress and trouble overwhelm you.

28

"Then they will call to me but I will not answer;
  they will look for me but will not find me,

29

since they hated knowledge
  and did not choose to fear the Lord.

30

Since they would not accept my advice
  and spurned my rebuke,

31

they will eat the fruit of their ways
  and be filled with the fruit of their schemes.

32

For the waywardness of the simple will kill them,
  and the complacency of fools will destroy them;

33

but whoever listens to me will live in safety and be at ease, without fear
of harm.

CHAPTER 2

Seek the love of God!!

"But from there you will seek the Lord your God and you will find him, if you search after him with all your heart and with all your soul." (English Standard Version, Deuteronomy 4:29)

D o you know what your purpose is while you are here on earth? Let me help you out. You were made to be examples of Jesus Christ here on Earth. Living by his word, spreading the gospel to those who do not know him. Being the example while experiencing trials and tests to see if you make it into eternity in the kingdom of heaven after your flesh is no longer viable for this earth. Earth is your temporary assignment, not your destination. Do not fall in love with the things of the world. This world is full of sinful behavior. As a believer of Jesus Christ, you are constantly tested to see if you will receive your rewards in Heaven based on how you live your life. Think of earth as practice test for the real thing. You get to choose how you want to live for eternity. Hot in hell or chilling in the kingdom of the Lord. Should I say more? I do not know about you, but I do not like being hot. My make-up runs and my hair sweats so I look a hot mess on a hot day as if I just jumped out of the shower and that is literally just walking around. That is not the way I want to live for eternity. You know where I am not trying to go. What about you? Be mindful, your actions may end up deciding for you.

God allows us free will to make our own choices every day. We all learn what is right and wrong as toddlers. Some of us choose to do wrong because it is either fun, feels good or we do not know any better. Only when you begin to choose the way of the word will you begin to make good choices. Think about it, you are born into sin, so it is a good possibility that you will have to experience bad choices before you finally decide to make better choices for your life. That time may not come until you have repeatedly made bad choices, putting yourself in a situation where the only way out is to look up. No one can judge you. Whenever that time comes do not worry. Have faith that God got you because He has been patiently waiting just for you. He is excited that His daughter is deciding to seek Him. If you have not experienced any hardship in life, it is either because you are running with the devil, or your time is coming. You are not exempt, boo. It will come, just live a little bit longer and you will experience some trials. That is why God sent this book, to help you get your armor ready for what is about to come.

Some of you have become bruised or broken by your past, fearful of your future and misguided with the present. At times, you do not know where to turn. Your father in Heaven wants to be there for you in your time of need. He just wants you to seek Him voluntarily. So, he knows you are making a choice to choose him. He is always with you, but no one wants to feel forced to do anything. Think about it. Forced decisions most times lead to deception. I say that because, if someone forces you to do something, whatever it is. There will be no compassion, love, thoughtfulness, or positive emotions behind it because it was not your own choice. On the other hand, when you want something, your heart is overwhelmed with Joy when you receive it. Example: Choosing to go to bible study verses your parents making you go. Chose Jesus!

This is what the Lord wants from you. He wants you to seek Him with your whole heart. Just call on Him and He is there. Seek Him and He will find you. Ask Him and He will provide. In His timing for your life of course. Remember, He created you for His Glory. He will never leave you in any situation He has not prepared you for, so when something comes up that you are not prepared for, then you should ask the Lord for help. Knock and He will answer. With open arms, He has been waiting all along, just for you. All for your benefit. The Lord only wants to bring great things into your life. Who better to ask for things then from your father? Everything that you lack, need or desire will be given to you from the Lord.

That love that you are missing and have been searching for is from your father in Heaven. You will not find this kind of love from anyone on Earth. He is waiting to shower you with all His love because you are His child. Some of you do not even know what you are searching for. *Spoiler Alert*: It is the unconditional, everlasting, unexplainable love of God. He says every need and desire of your heart will be given to you when you begin to obey His word.

The Lord is not expecting you to be perfect and not make mistakes throughout life. No one is perfect but God. But when you do make a bad decision, repent, which is ask for forgiveness, and try your best not to commit the same mistake again. God knows you will make the same mistake over and over until you realize it and decide to change. That is why He says:

"Judge not, and you will not be judged; condemn not, and you will not be condemned; forgive, and you will be forgiven" (Douay-Rheims 1899 American Edition (DRA), Luke 6:37)

Just as you will make the same mistake over and over, others will, too. So, show them the same grace as the Lord has shown to you. The Lord is waiting for you to humble yourself and understand you cannot live this life on your own. You need help and He is willing and ready to help. All you must do is ask.

Prayer: Father God, I come to you with open arms and a humble heart. I seek your face today and I know that with you all things are possible for those who believe. I believe in your word, Lord. I trust you, Lord. Come into my life and guide me to you, Lord. I want to build a father-daughter relationship with you lord. I love you and I thank you. In Jesus name, Amen.

New International Version, Proverbs 2

Moral Benefits of Wisdom

1.

My son, if you accept my words
   and store up my commands within you,

2

turning your ear to wisdom
   and applying your heart to understanding—

3

indeed, if you call out for insight
   and cry aloud for understanding,

4

and if you look for it as for silver
   and search for it as for hidden treasure,

5

then you will understand the fear of the Lord
   and find the knowledge of God.

6

For the Lord gives wisdom;
   from his mouth come knowledge and understanding.

7

He holds success in store for the upright, non serving service j
   he is a shield to those whose walk is blameless,

8 for he guards the course of the just
   and protects the way of his faithful ones.

9

Then you will understand what is right and just
   and fair—every good path.

10

For wisdom will enter your heart,
   and knowledge will be pleasant to your soul.

11

Discretion will protect you,
   and understanding will guard you.

12
Wisdom will save you from the ways of wicked men,
   from men whose words are perverse,
13
who have left the straight paths
   to walk in dark ways,
14
who delight in doing wrong
   and rejoice in the perverseness of evil,
15
whose paths are crooked
   and who are devious in their ways.
16
Wisdom will save you also from the adulterous woman,
   from the wayward woman with her seductive words,
17
who has left the partner of her youth
   and ignored the covenant she made before God.[a]
18
Surely her house leads down to death
   and her paths to the spirits of the dead.
19
None who go to her return
   or attain the paths of life.
20
Thus you will walk in the ways of the good
   and keep to the paths of the righteous.
21
For the upright will live in the land,
   and the blameless will remain in it;
22
but the wicked will be cut off from the land,
   and the unfaithful will be torn from it.

CHAPTER 3

It's all a part of God's Plan

Long before you were even thought about, God gave you a purpose. He made sure you looked the way you were designed to look and speak the way you speak; He chose your parents for you because He has a plan for your life. Your purpose will not be revealed until you experience and learn the necessary tools needed to carry out that purpose. You will not understand why you go through the things you will go through until it's over. So, as you go through situations and trials, go through them with an expectation that it's for a purpose and you're going to need whatever you gain from the event later in life. You're gathering all of the ingredients for a cake; Not until you have the flour, the eggs, the sugar, milk, butter, salt, vanilla extract, nutmeg, and the whipping cream will you be able to carry out the plan to make the cake. So, sit back, be grateful, and praise the Lord at every chance because He is the author of your story. It is all a part of His plan for your life.

When the Lord places a thought or an idea upon you, do not brush it off- it is a part of His plan for you. Follow through with it, even if it seems unattainable at the time. My grandpa, Allen Pugh, told me that you set out for a mission, and you don't abandon the mission, you follow through with the mission until the mission is complete. Regardless of how impossible it may seem, if the mission is from the Lord, the Lord will make a way out of what seems to be no way. I can personally attest to that. Never doubt what the Lord can do if you ask Him. He will always show up and show out-humble yourself, allow the Lord to guide you and understand that this life was not meant for us to live on our own. Our father made it so if you seek Him and acknowledge Him, He will make sure you accomplish what He has set for your life. He will lead you down the righteous path if you decide to follow his way.

There will be times that we want things that are not for us, and we go after them, then we get mad when they do not work out. Remember, most times it's because you are either thinking too small because God has something greater for your life or you aren't mentally prepared for what you are asking for. Being mentally prepared is key. So, go through your trials and obstacles because everything you go through is a part of God's plan for your life, the good and the bad. When you persist and continue to follow through with the things that are not for you, they may be good for a little while but everything that shimmers isn't gold. Like the saying goes - all money is not good money. So true.

The Lord will never lead you astray. Trust in His commands. For example: You might be in a situation where you have been waiting for a job, you have been applying to all these places, you want this one job, and you get an interview for what you think is your dream job at this specific company. You pray on it the night before the interview. You go into the interview and everything you thought about this company is right-the money is right, the commute is far but worth it to you, your income would be awesome-but something within you tells you not to take it. You ignore the inner voice and take the job. That job brings you nothing but stress and drama. This is where trusting in the Lord and trusting yourself comes into play.

Listen to the small voice inside, it is God trying to warn you about something. How many times have you said something told me to do that, or I knew I should've? You better start listening to those "something told me" moments. Do not be the person who is always saying dang, something told me not to or to do this. If you do listen to the Lord's warnings and do not take the job, watch how God blesses you with a better opportunity with more benefits, more income, less commute and little to no stress or drama. Moral of the story, listen, trust, and wait on the Lord. He knows best. His plans are so much bigger than we could ever expect. Until Jesus is the only name you can call on, you will never know how much you need him.

Prayer: Thank you Lord, for not allowing me to have what I thought I wanted but supplying me with what I need. Lord, begin to open my eyes so I will be able to see what you have in store for me and not just what is physically in front of me. In Jesus name, Amen.

New International Version, Proverbs

Wisdom Bestows Well-Being
1
My son, do not forget my teaching,
   but keep my commands in your heart,
2
for they will prolong your life many years
   and bring you peace and prosperity.
3
Let love and faithfulness never leave you;
   bind them around your neck,
   write them on the tablet of your heart.
4
Then you will win favor and a good name
   in the sight of God and man.
5
Trust in the Lord with all your heart
   and lean not on your own understanding;
6
in all your ways submit to him,
   and he will make your paths straight. [a]
7
Do not be wise in your own eyes;
   fear the Lord and shun evil.

8
This will bring health to your body
  and nourishment to your bones.
9
Honor the Lord with your wealth,
  with the first fruits of all your crops;
10
then your barns will be filled to overflowing,
  and your vats will brim over with new wine.
11
My son, do not despise the Lord's discipline,
  and do not resent his rebuke,
12
because the Lord disciplines those he loves,
  as a father the son he delights in.[b]
13
Blessed are those who find wisdom,
  those who gain understanding,
14
for she is more profitable than silver
  and yields better returns than gold.
15
She is more precious than rubies;
  nothing you desire can compare with her.
16
Long life is in her right hand;
  in her left hand are riches and honor.
17
Her ways are pleasant ways,
  and all her paths are peace.
18
She is a tree of life to those who take hold of her;
  those who hold her fast will be blessed.
19
By wisdom the Lord laid the earth's foundations,
  by understanding he set the heavens in place;

20

by his knowledge the watery depths were divided,
    and the clouds let drop the dew.

21

My son, do not let wisdom and understanding out of your sight,
    preserve sound judgment and discretion;

22

they will be life for you,
    an ornament to grace your neck.

23

Then you will go on your way in safety,
    and your foot will not stumble.

24

When you lie down, you will not be afraid;
    when you lie down, your sleep will be sweet.

25

Have no fear of sudden disaster
    or of the ruin that overtakes the wicked,

26

for the Lord will be at your side
    and will keep your foot from being snared.

27

Do not withhold good from those to whom it is due,
    when it is in your power to act.

28

Do not say to your neighbor,
    "Come back tomorrow and I'll give it to you"—
    when you already have it with you.

29

Do not plot harm against your neighbor,
    who lives trustfully near you.

30

Do not accuse anyone for no reason—
    when they have done you no harm.

31

Do not envy the violent
  or choose any of their ways.

32

For the Lord detests the perverse
  but takes the upright into his confidence.

33

The Lord's curse is on the house of the wicked,
  but he blesses the home of the righteous.

34

He mocks proud mockers
  but shows favor to the humble and oppressed.

35

The wise inherit honor,
  but fools get only shame.

CHAPTER 4

There is a reason for everything!

D o you believe that your life was already planned before your parents even knew each other? Well, it is true. God put you here f or a reason and a purpose. Every one of us will go through things to realize the only one who will ever have our back, always and never give up on us is our father in heaven. Until you reach this understanding you will go through things and wonder why this is happening to me. Our lives are a jigsaw puzzle without the box. You do not know what the picture will be but, once you're complete, it will be beautiful, and it will all make sense. Every piece of our life's puzzle is needed. Everything you go through, the people you meet, the pickles you get stuck in, the good and the bad all are needed to mold you into who God is preparing you to become. The Devil initiates trials and obstacles to attack your faith, but they will not destroy you. They may make you feel as though you are being set back from your goals, based on how you react to the situations. Although some of those situations maybe difficult to handle, just pray through it because pain is temporary.

We always try to make sense of why things happen, but things happen when they are supposed to happen. Timing is everything! Everything happens on God's timing. It is a matter of when God allows it to happen or not. Sometimes we get upset because things do not happen on our time or when we want them to but, sit back and really think about it-were you mentally ready for what you had asked for, that you have not received yet?

God is tickled when we think things are not lining up with our plans, because he already has bigger plans prepared for us.

Do not get mad and feel like things should have played out differently because you never know what the Lord has prepared for your future. He promises to give you the desires of your heart and provide your every need if you obey His word. Growing up my dream was to become a nurse like my mom, my mom is great with people and everybody she meets instantly falls in love with her. She is still my role model to this day. You are such a loving, kind-hearted and all-around wonderful person, I am so thankful for you. I love you, Mommy. Shout out to Teresa Simpson. So let me tell ya'll my plan, I thought I was going to go to nursing school, graduate, take the nursing boards exam, pass with flying colors and apply for a hospital job and become financially stable as a Nurse. My plan was clearly not big enough, so after I received my Bachelor of Science in Nursing, I took the test 7 times, not able to pass, I began to get frustrated because I thought it was a setting me back from my plans. What I didn't see was, God aligning me with the right people and skills to be able to carry out my purpose He created for me. Not the one I created for myself. Looking back, what it did was open my eyes to other areas in which I could prosper when I receive my Nursing License. I needed a little but more knowledge to be able to follow through with the plan. While experiencing what I believed then was a setback, I was introduced to other ways that the Lord wants me to help His people. While showing me, which of His people to help, my purpose is not to take care of the sick individuals in the hospital who may be on their way to see Him but to heal and edify our future generations to come. I became a Certified Life Coach in the process and realized the skills I acquired during nursing school are needed in my current position where I currently work as well as with my non-profit organization that the Lord has prompted me to create. Look at God! Turning it all around for my good and He will do the same for you. I would not have learned the valuable information and received the connections, I needed working anywhere else. I was supposed to be in this position at this moment in time to receive everything I have received. While still being able to help people in more ways than I ever imagined. What I thought was a "setback" was a "set up for a comeback" – Willie Jolly. I wasn't ready for what I asked for so He had to slow me down and prepare me for the goodness He has stored up for me. The Lord will turn what you think is bad into something great. Trust in the Lord with all your heart and he will not fail you.

Everybody will have a testimony to share and your testimony will inspire someone one day, so do not judge anyone based on what they have been through to get to where they are. There is a reason behind everything. God does not promise life will be easy or that you will not encounter the enemy, but he does say that He will not allow you to go through anything alone, He will never leave you as you go through it. Go through your tough times with grace, being thankful with prayer and knowing when it's over God will use all obstacles for your good because He is a Good, Good, Father.

Prayer: Thank you, Lord for allowing me to go through all that I have been though to get me where you need me to be. I trust you, Lord. In Jesus name, Amen.

New International Version, Proverbs 4

Get Wisdom at Any Cost
1
Listen, my sons, to a father's instruction;
    pay attention and gain understanding.
2
I give you sound learning,
    so do not forsake my teaching.
3
For I too was a son to my father,
    still tender, and cherished by my mother.
4
Then he taught me, and he said to me,
    "Take hold of my words with all your heart;
    keep my commands, and you will live.

5
Get wisdom, get understanding;
  do not forget my words or turn away from them.
6
Do not forsake wisdom, and she will protect you;
  love her, and she will watch over you.
7
The beginning of wisdom is this: Get[a] wisdom.
  Though it cost all you have,[b] get understanding.
8
Cherish her, and she will exalt you;
  embrace her, and she will honor you.
9
She will give you a garland to grace your head
  and present you with a glorious crown."
10
Listen, my son, accept what I say,
  and the years of your life will be many.
11
I instruct you in the way of wisdom
  and lead you along straight paths.
12
When you walk, your steps will not be hampered;
  when you run, you will not stumble.
13
Hold on to instruction, do not let it go;
  guard it well, for it is your life.
14
Do not set foot on the path of the wicked
  or walk in the way of evildoers.
15
Avoid it, do not travel on it;
  turn from it and go on your way.
16
For they cannot rest until they do evil;
  they are robbed of sleep till they make someone stumble.

17

They eat the bread of wickedness
   and drink the wine of violence.

18

The path of the righteous is like the morning sun,
   shining ever brighter till the full light of day.

19

But the way of the wicked is like deep darkness;
   they do not know what makes them stumble.

20

My son, pay attention to what I say;
   turn your ear to my words.

21

Do not let them out of your sight,
   keep them within your heart;

22

for they are life to those who find them
   and health to one's whole body.

23

Above all else, guard your heart,
   for everything you do flows from it.

24

Keep your mouth free of perversity;
   keep corrupt talk far from your lips.

25

Let your eyes look straight ahead;
   fix your gaze directly before you.

26

Give careful thought to the[c] paths for your feet
   and be steadfast in all your ways.

27

Do not turn to the right or the left;
   keep your foot from evil.

CHAPTER 5

Obey Your Parents

(New International Version, Ephesians 6:1), *"Children obey your parents in the lord for this is right."*

Parents are given to us to help guide us through life. The parents we get are chosen by the Lord. Not all parents are good parents, but we must respect them as our parents anyway. You only get one set; you cannot exchange them. Some of you only have close adults to turn to or no parents at all. So, value those parent-figures and/or parents that you have in your life. Be grateful and thankful for them everyday. Remember this: parents are human too, meaning they make mistakes, let you down, and maybe mean at times. It's ok. God gives us grace and mercy, so you must give them some, too.

I used to dislike my father for not being in my life when I needed him but as I got older, I realized that he was 18 years old when he became a father. He did not know what being a father entailed until he was older, and I had already resented him. It took a while to rebuild our relationship and when I did, he was not in the best shape and passed away some years later. To this day I wish I would have never allowed my mother's personal issues with my dad affect how I viewed him because their relationship had nothing to do with me, I could have had what I needed which was a father/daughter relationship with my biological father before it was too late. So, forgive your parents of their short comings and mistakes they may have made. Let it go!! Start to rebuild your relationships today. Tomorrow is not promised.

Just as parents know what their children are capable of, our father, Lord and Savior Jesus Christ knows each of us. Down to how many hairs He placed on each of our heads. Just as your parents have watched you grow, watched how you interact with others, and we see how you respond to situations. No one knows you better than your father in heaven. As a teenager, you may think your parents are holding you back from fun or trying to ruin your life, but reality is they are trying to prevent what they have been through from happening to you. The world is full of sin baby girl. When you are born you are born into sin. Parents are supposed to protect you as best as they can, but sometimes they do not always do a good job at it. Whatever they do tell you, listen, because the real world is cruel and will eat you alive spiritually, mentally, emotionally, and yes even physically if you are not properly prepared. The adults in your life are trying to properly prepare you to prevent you from saying, I should have listened when my mom tried to tell me .... you fill in the blank.

Parents are placed in your life because we all need guidance, proper nurturing, love, rules, and discipline to respect and appreciate things and people we encounter throughout our life. Life is all about making choices one bad choice could ruin your life and even one bad choice made by someone you are with. Parents are supposed to be here to show you how to build a relationship with the Father in Heaven. Being obedient to his word is the only way to go about making decisions, so that you will not continue to make the wrong ones. Although, as kids, the best way to learn is through experience, your parents will always try to prevent you from failure, hurt, harm and danger, it comes as human nature to protect your young.

Although, some parents do not seek Christ before they have kids, it's up to every person to build their own relationship with the Lord. Once you find out about the love, he has in store for you, begin to seek him as well. This should be the motto for all parents but as we said earlier parents are human as well. Proverbs 22:6 (NIV) which says, *"Train a child up in the way they should go and when he is old, he will not depart from it."* Your parents can say "do as I say and not as I do" but history shows regardless of what your parents tell you, 8 out of 10 times you repeat the actions your see. It is up to you to make the decision to follow what is being shown to you. You will have to go through and accept the consequences of your choices for everything you do. Take time when making choices. Life is not about what happens to you but how you respond to what has happened to you. You are in control of only one thing: your actions. If you follow Christ, everything will work out for your good. The Bible says in the New International Version, Ecclesiastes 3:1 *"There is a time for everything and a season for every activity under the heavens."* So, do not rush through life you will miss the good times. Learn to enjoy the moment as it is happening. You are only a child for 18 years. You will have many years to live life not under your given parents' rules, just remember that your father in heaven has rules as well.

Prayer for today: Heavenly father, help me to be wise in making the best decisions for my life so that it will be for your good. In Jesus' name, Amen.

(New International Version, Proverbs 5)

Warning Against Adultery
1
My son, pay attention to my wisdom,
    turn your ear to my words of insight,
2
that you may maintain discretion
    and your lips may preserve knowledge.
3
For the lips of the adulterous woman drip honey,
    and her speech is smoother than oil;
4
but in the end she is bitter as gall,
    sharp as a double-edged sword.

5
Her feet go down to death;
  her steps lead straight to the grave.
6
She gives no thought to the way of life;
  her paths wander aimlessly, but she does not know it.
7
Now then, my sons, listen to me;
  do not turn aside from what I say.
8
Keep to a path far from her,
  do not go near the door of her house,
9
lest you lose your honor to others
  and your dignity[a] to one who is cruel,
10
lest strangers feast on your wealth
  and your toil enrich the house of another.
11
At the end of your life you will groan,
  when your flesh and body are spent.
12
You will say, "How I hated discipline!
  How my heart spurned correction!
13
I would not obey my teachers
  or turn my ear to my instructors.
14
And I was soon in serious trouble
  in the assembly of God's people."
15
Drink water from your own cistern,
  running water from your own well.
16
Should your springs overflow in the streets,
  your streams of water in the public squares?

17
Let them be yours alone,
  never to be shared with strangers.
18
May your fountain be blessed,
  and may you rejoice in the wife of your youth.
19 A loving doe, a graceful deer—
  may her breasts satisfy you always,
  may you ever be intoxicated with her love.
20
Why, my son, be intoxicated with another man's wife?
  Why embrace the bosom of a wayward woman?
21
For your ways are in full view of the Lord,
  and he examines all your paths.
22
The evil deeds of the wicked ensnare them;
  the cords of their sins hold them fast.
23
For lack of discipline they will die,
  led astray by their own great folly.

CHAPTER 6

Forgiveness

As we go through our own personal journeys, we all should be trying to achieve the same goal. To get on Heaven's list. The key to that is forgiveness. Forgiveness is something that is not easy to do but so necessary for growth and peace within yourself. To become more Christ like. You must learn what it means to forgive, why we forgive, and how to accomplish true forgiveness. In New International Version Matthew 18:21-22, Then Peter came to Jesus and asked, "Lord, how many times shall I forgive my brother or sister who sins against me? Up to seven times? Jesus answered, "I tell you, not seven but seventy-seven times. This does not mean if someone keeps messing up to stop forgiving them at 77 times but rather there is no limit to how many times you should forgive.

Your heart becomes hardened when you hold onto grudges and choose not to forgive. So, begin to seek the Lord to help heal your heart and allow the ability for you to forgive whoever has ever done wrong to you. You do not want to go around intentionally or unintentionally hurting people because you are hurt. The saying is very true: hurt people, hurt people. (People who have been hurt go on to hurt other people).

Forgiveness is a process. Let me clarify, just because you forgive someone does not mean you have to continue the relationship/friendship/communication with the person who hurt you. You forgive because Jesus forgave you for your sins before you were ever born. He died on the cross so that your sins would be forgiven. So, you too must forgive those who mistreat you and continue to do you wrong. You do not forgive them because they deserve it but because you did not deserve it when it was done for you. You forgive to lighten the burden off your chest.

What you do not want to happen is to let the enemy win by you choosing not to forgive people. Just think about it when you do not forgive you allow the bad memories to take control and replay over and over in your head which may cause depression, anger, anxiety, and pain. Even more reason you should want to let go and forgive. "How do you start to forgive" you might ask? Forgiveness can only be received when you decide to let go of the hurt, anger, or pain and give it to God. No matter what they did to you. Nothing is exempt. Everything can be forgiven. What if Jesus had a limitation on what he forgave us for. There might be no one in Heaven. I know I wouldn't be, so thank you, Lord, for forgiving me of my sins. Once you let it go, I mean really let it go and not just say I am good, but really mean it. The situation will no longer prick your heart. You no longer become angry when you speak about the situation but feel a sense of peace with whatever the outcome may be. That's when true freedom will appear. Another reason to forgive is because unforgiveness keeps you in bondage. Now, that's no way to live.

Once you truly forgive in your heart, you will receive your peace like never before. Then and only then can you begin to start your process of rebuilding trust. Not necessarily trust with the one who caused the pain but to the rest of the people around you. Believe it or not unforgiveness messes everything thing up for everybody. One bad apple does spoil the bunch. That one situation causes you to question everyone about everything. Now, that you have forgiven whoever for whatever they have caused, you know you can begin to trust again. Keep in mind, not everybody can be trusted, trust is earned. There will be some scenarios where you forgive for yourself and keep it moving, some people do not deserve second, third and fourth chances, to hurt you. They do not respect you or your chances so why waste your time. Pray on it and ask the Lord to show you discernment.

Shout out to my amazing spiritual father, Bishop Derek Grier of Grace Church in Dumfries, VA. Again, if you do not have a church home you are more than welcome to come to mine in person or watch online at www.gracechurchva.org. Bishop Grier has comprised these steps to building lost trust that I would like to share with you all. For the mendable relationships. You do not stay angry forever but delight to show mercy. (New International Version Micah 7:18)

* Say What You Mean and Mean What You Say: Be clear and honor your commitments and over time your track record will speak for itself! Keep your word, no matter how small.
* Be Consistent because trust is built over time: Love is unconditional, but trust can only be earned or lost.
* Be Transparent: Admit mistakes and be open, even when it is uncomfortable.
* Show Respect: You may be right, but was your delivery kind? Everything has a way of being said without hurting the next person's feelings, but there are some things that do not need to be said. Ask the lord for wisdom and understanding through these tough times to help you see things from not only your point of view but others as well.

Prayer: Jesus, thank you for dying for my sins. I ask that you provide me with strength to help me to forgive my wrong doers, love my enemies, and be at peace in my spirit. In Jesus name, Amen.

New International Version, Proverbs 6

Warnings Against Folly

1

My son, if you have put up security for your neighbor,
    if you have shaken hands in pledge for a stranger,

2

you have been trapped by what you said,
    ensnared by the words of your mouth.

3
So do this, my son, to free yourself,
    since you have fallen into your neighbor's hands:
Go—to the point of exhaustion—[a]
    and give your neighbor no rest!
4
Allow no sleep to your eyes,
    no slumber to your eyelids.
5
Free yourself, like a gazelle from the hand of the hunter,
    like a bird from the snare of the fowler.
6
Go to the ant, you sluggard;
    consider its ways and be wise!
7
It has no commander,
    no overseer or ruler,
8
yet it stores its provisions in summer
    and gathers its food at harvest.
9
How long will you lie there, you sluggard?
    When will you get up from your sleep?
10
A little sleep, a little slumber,
    a little folding of the hands to rest—
11
and poverty will come on you like a thief
    and scarcity like an armed man.
12
A troublemaker and a villain,
    who goes about with a corrupt mouth,
13
    who winks maliciously with his eye,
    signals with his feet
    and motions with his fingers,

14
    who plots evil with deceit in his heart—
    he always stirs up conflict.

15
Therefore disaster will overtake him in an instant;
    he will suddenly be destroyed—without remedy.

16
There are six things the Lord hates,
    seven that are detestable to him:

a lying tongue,
hands that shed innocent blood,

feet that are quick to rush into evil,

and a person who stirs up conflict in the community.
Warning Against Adultery

20
My son, keep your father's command
    and do not forsake your mother's teaching.

21
Bind them always on your heart;
    fasten them around your neck.

22
When you walk, they will guide you;
    when you sleep, they will watch over you;
    when you awake, they will speak to you.

23
For this command is a lamp,
    this teaching is a light,
and correction and instruction
    are the way to life,

24
keeping you from your neighbor's wife,
    from the smooth talk of a wayward woman.

25
Do not lust in your heart after her beauty
  or let her captivate you with her eyes.
26
For a prostitute can be had for a loaf of bread,
  but another man's wife preys on your very life.
27
Can a man scoop fire into his lap
  without his clothes being burned?
28
Can a man walk on hot coals
  without his feet being scorched?
29
So is he who sleeps with another man's wife;
  no one who touches her will go unpunished.
30
People do not despise a thief if he steals
  to satisfy his hunger when he is starving.
31
Yet if he is caught, he must pay sevenfold,
  though it costs him all the wealth of his house.
32
But a man who commits adultery has no sense;
  whoever does so destroys himself.
33
Blows and disgrace are his lot,
  and his shame will never be wiped away.
34
For jealousy arouses a husband's fury,
  and he will show no mercy when he takes revenge.
35
He will not accept any compensation;
  he will refuse a bribe, however great it is.

Love Yourself

CHAPTER 7

Speak affirmations over your life!

Repeat X 3 I am a child of God, he has promised me a prosperous future.

Good Morning, Boo! How are you doing today? Did you remember to thank the Lord for waking you up and blessing you with another day to be a blessing to someone else? Did you look in the mirror and speak truth to yourself today? Speak positive things over your life, so positive results will follow. The purpose of an affirmation is to build confidence and belief what you are saying about yourself. It is a positive statement or goal in its completed state. We must build ourselves up because not all of us have parents who speak great things about us or into our lives. Do not rely on anyone else to build you up as you go through life, no one else is going to do it but you. Speak them with confidence and believe it with all you heart, knowing this is how you feel, and it is true. Once you create your own personal affirmations speak them aloud every morning to start you off on the right track. They are especially needed during times of pain, weakness, depression, grief, mourning, and when you're feeling unmotivated. This will give you a little pick-me-up, so you feel nothing is too hard for you obtain.

Take the time to write down or type in your notes on your phone and make up your own, here's an example of what I started telling my daughters until they created their own. Stand tall and say it aloud in the mirror: I am a child of the most high God, I am beautiful, I am valuable, I am important, I am smart, I am ambitious, I deserve respect, I will succeed in whatever I put my mind to, I am an excellent reader, I do not give up, I love math, I obey my parents and I know God loves me, he is always with me, He will protect me and keep me safe. No matter what trials, obstacles, or temptations I may face, Lord I know you will be with me. Lord, I know with you all things are possible. Say them with boldness from your gut. The truth is God has your best interest at heart. He wants you to be the best version of you and knowledgeable of the events that may happen in life so when you encounter life's scenarios you will be equipped with the right tools to make the best decision on how to defeat the enemy. The enemy preys on your weakness. He wants your guard to be down so he can creep up and overtake your soul. Affirmations are a part of your defense mechanism. If you speak it, you will begin to believe it and then you will become it. So again, speak positivity over your life. "You can do all things through Him who gives you strength." New international version Philippines 4:13

Prayer: Lord, thank you for this day, I ask that you give me the strength to endure the obstacles I will face this day forward. Help me to believe what I am saying so it can be engraved into my heart. In Jesus name, Amen.

Proverbs 7

Warning Against the Adulterous Woman
1
My son, keep my words
    and store up my commands within you.
2
Keep my commands and you will live;
    guard my teachings as the apple of your eye.

3
Bind them on your fingers;
    write them on the tablet of your heart.

4
Say to wisdom, "You are my sister,"
    and to insight, "You are my relative."

5
They will keep you from the adulterous woman,
    from the wayward woman with her seductive words.

6
At the window of my house
    I looked down through the lattice.

7
I saw among the simple,
    I noticed among the young men,
    a youth who had no sense.

8 He was going down the street near her corner,
    walking along in the direction of her house

9
at twilight, as the day was fading,
    as the dark of night set in.

10
Then out came a woman to meet him,
    dressed like a prostitute and with crafty intent.

11
(She is unruly and defiant,
    her feet never stay at home;

12
now in the street, now in the squares,
    at every corner she lurks.)

13
She took hold of him and kissed him
    and with a brazen face she said:

14
"Today I fulfilled my vows,
   and I have food from my fellowship offering at home.
15
So I came out to meet you;
   I looked for you and have found you!
16 I have covered my bed
   with colored linens from Egypt.
17
I have perfumed my bed
   with myrrh, aloes and cinnamon.
18
Come, let's drink deeply of love till morning;
   let's enjoy ourselves with love!
19
My husband is not at home;
   he has gone on a long journey.
20
He took his purse filled with money
   and will not be home till full moon."
21
With persuasive words she led him astray;
   she seduced him with her smooth talk.
22
All at once he followed her
   like an ox going to the slaughter,
like a deer[a] stepping into a noose[b]
23
   till an arrow pierces his liver,
like a bird darting into a snare,
   little knowing it will cost him his life.
24
Now then, my sons, listen to me;
   pay attention to what I say.

25

Do not let your heart turn to her ways
  or stray into her paths.

26

Many are the victims she has brought down;
  her slain are a mighty throng.

27

Her house is a highway to the grave,
  leading down to the chambers of death.

CHAPTER 8

Coping with life changes

God does not promise that we will not experience pain, hurt or trials but, he does promise as we go through it, he will never leave us. When you go through traumatic events in your life, go through them with the expectation of change once they are over. Then we must get realigned to the new reality because what was reality before the event is no longer how life is going to be. Change means, a new way of thinking should be formed. The way you thought before is no longer how you should think. To be able to be effective with coping with traumatic events or sudden unwanted changes is to go through a process. Every event that severely impacts your life should be handled as a grief. Grief is defined as a deep sorrow or loss. Grief can affect you physically, mentally, spiritually, behaviorally, and personally. To overcome grief is a process here is how to begin the process.

There are 5 stages of grief and loss which are: 1. Denial and isolation; 2. Anger; 3. Bargaining; 4. Depression; 5. Acceptance. People who are grieving do not necessarily go through these stages in the same order or they may even experience multiple stages at once. In order to fully recover from grief we all have to go through these processes so that we can learn, grow and begin to apply what you learned to life. The severity of the event is what determines how we will ultimately handle a situation. Trust the process. If you can't seem to do it on your own then seek counseling. It's always good to talk to someone outside of close friends or family.

Denial is the first stage. Usually everyone denies they are going through something until it becomes their reality. Realize what the reality of the situation is and do not be naïve to the facts. It is funny how we don't know that we deserve to be treated better but people looking from the outside can. Believe what you are shown and believe when people show you who they are.

Anger begins when you realize what you are going through and become upset with the factors that lead to it. This may be a stage where we get stuck and take longer to transition from. Beware. Do not get stuck here. It is ok to be angry but then begin to let go and let God handle it. Anger is when you talk about the situation and it's still able to get you ferrous. To let go, do not talk about it, or go places that will remind you or bring the memories of the situation to you. Avoid walking down memory lane. You will be angry until you reach peace. Always remember, it is ok to cry, you have to let it out.

Bargaining is when we start making requests to the Lord. "Father God if you do this, I will do this." Hopelessly, trying to plead your case to the Lord. Instead of bargaining, begin to pray and ask the lord to show you what he needs you to do. To heal from this and show you how to handle this situation better the next time. Trust there will be a next time.

Depression may be the phase where most people get stuck in and fail to progress to the next phase if they do not have a relationship with the Lord. Praying and asking for strength to endure at this time is what will pull you through. You can be depressed and not know you are depressed. During this phase you will talk about what happened often. It will have progressed from anger to hurt or sadness. During this time, ask the Lord to help you to forgive whoever for whatever. So that peace can begin to form and soften your heart. This phase may take the longest to complete. Maybe even years. It takes constant prayer and trust in the Lord to get through this phase but once you get there, you will start to feel so much peace in your heart.

Acceptance is when you have a sense of peace with whatever the outcome. You conclude that whether it ends up in your favor or not, that it was a part of God's plan. This is when you can honestly say, "I am ok with the outcome." You will know when you reach this phase in the process, when everything that you once worried about or feared to happen or was mad at, no longer makes you angry or upset. Hopefully, you can look back at the situation and say what did I learn from it and take what you learned and apply it in the next phases of your life. Everything you go through is to teach you for the future. View every situation as a learning lesson.

Some of you may go through these stages in a different order; that is ok. You maybe even revisit a phase; we all are different and learn differently. Some of you may go through these phases quickly, some of you may never go through some stages or they maybe combined, some get stuck and some people never reach acceptance. Which brings them to lifelong depression, unbelief, bitterness, and anger issues. That is why we are not to judge our sisters, because we all go through these same phases at different points in life. Have mercy for others because it is right and because we do not know what issues other people are dealing with.

Go through situations with faith knowing that God got you!! Stay in faith and believe it is something better on the other side of the hurt because it is. God promised he will be with you, not that he will have it avoid you because after all, to learn you must experience it firsthand.

Prayer: Thank you, Lord for allowing my hurt to force me to grow in ways I cannot explain. Only you know where my journey will end. I submit to you. I trust you, Lord. Lead me into your righteousness. In Jesus name, Amen.

Proverbs 8

Wisdom's Call
8
Does not wisdom call out?
    Does not understanding raise her voice?
2
At the highest point along the way,
    where the paths meet, she takes her stand;

3

beside the gate leading into the city,
     at the entrance, she cries aloud:

4

"To you, O people, I call out;
     I raise my voice to all mankind.

5

You who are simple, gain prudence;
     you who are foolish, set your hearts on it.[a]

6

Listen, for I have trustworthy things to say;
     I open my lips to speak what is right.

7

My mouth speaks what is true,
     for my lips detest wickedness.

8

All the words of my mouth are just;
     none of them is crooked or perverse.

9

To the discerning all of them are right;
     they are upright to those who have found knowledge.

10

Choose my instruction instead of silver,
     knowledge rather than choice gold,

11

for wisdom is more precious than rubies,
     and nothing you desire can compare with her.

12

"I, wisdom, dwell together with prudence;
     I possess knowledge and discretion.

13

To fear the Lord is to hate evil;
     I hate pride and arrogance,
     evil behavior and perverse speech.

14
Counsel and sound judgment are mine;
   I have insight, I have power.
15
By me kings reign
   and rulers issue decrees that are just;
16
by me princes govern,
   and nobles—all who rule on earth.[b]
17
I love those who love me,
   and those who seek me find me.
18
With me are riches and honor,
   enduring wealth and prosperity.
19
My fruit is better than fine gold;
   what I yield surpasses choice silver.
20
I walk in the way of righteousness,
   along the paths of justice,
21
bestowing a rich inheritance on those who love me
   and making their treasuries full.
22
"The Lord brought me forth as the first of his works,[c][d]
   before his deeds of old;
23
I was formed long ages ago,
   at the very beginning, when the world came to be.
24
When there were no watery depths, I was given birth,
   when there were no springs overflowing with water;
25 before the mountains were settled in place,
   before the hills, I was given birth,

26

before he made the world or its fields
  or any of the dust of the earth.

27

I was there when he set the heavens in place,
  when he marked out the horizon on the face of the deep,

28

when he established the clouds above
  and fixed securely the fountains of the deep,

29

when he gave the sea its boundary
  so the waters would not overstep his command,
and when he marked out the foundations of the earth.

30

  Then I was constantly[e] at his side.
I was filled with delight day after day,
  rejoicing always in his presence,

31

rejoicing in his whole world
  and delighting in mankind.

32

"Now then, my children, listen to me;
  blessed are those who keep my ways.

33

Listen to my instruction and be wise;
  do not disregard it.

34

Blessed are those who listen to me,
  watching daily at my doors,
  waiting at my doorway.

35

For those who find me find life
  and receive favor from the Lord.

36

But those who fail to find me harm themselves;
  all who hate me love death."

CHAPTER 9

Love yourself

Repeat: God loves me! I trust you Lord!

Hey Baby Girl, if you do not take anything else from this book, embrace this chapter. Remember It is ok to be alone. When you are alone, you learn things about yourself, the things that sometimes are not realized because of dependency of others or outside distractions. Alone time is also time that can be spent with God.

First, learn yourself. Learn who you are in Christ while learning what makes you cry, happy, mad, sad, what are you pet peeves, what are you afraid of, what motivates you, are you a procrastinator, what are your values, morals, do you keep your word, what do you enjoy doing, what are you good at, what is a great quality about you, what's something you need to work on, all of these are things that when you figure out about yourself, you have a choice to change it if you feel you want to or embrace your individuality. These personal questions help to build your confidence as well. The girl who knows what she stands for will not fall for anything.

Second, pray continually, Prayer really works. Pray and believe and the desires of your heart will be given to you. Praying is just talking to God. Talk to him in your own way. Read scripture back to him if you do not know what to say, the lord loves for you to speak what he has promised you and always speak from your heart.

Third, spend this time and focus on school events, school sports, getting your education, and doing the things that make you happy. Focusing on the wrong thing will distract you and prevent you from many experiences you need to have to build you as a person. An example: If you do not know what I mean, say you wanted to go to a basketball game, but your friends did not want to go so you decide not to go, you will end up missing the highlights of high school because of someone else's decisions. Go alone, learn to be ok with going places and doing things alone. Life is based on memories, the good, the bad, the funny, and the sad. Build memories. Enjoy being a child and have fun, you will have enough time to be an adult. Trust me! Time flies!

Fourth, no matter what anybody says about you, you are perfectly and wonderfully made. Love everything about you, even what people may make fun of you for. The Lord made you perfect. Embrace every part of you so you will be able to enjoy life and love yourself. God gave us free will, so you can decide to change personal characteristics about yourself, if you feel they need to be changed to be a better person. Become the person you want to be remembered as.

Fifth, Reflection is not something that everyone learns how to do but learn this early and it is a powerful tool. You reflect on situations to learn from them. Reflection is when you look back at situations after your emotions are no longer dictating your actions. Take the time and think about how you could have handled that situation differently to receive a different result. Think of the positive takeaways and apply those to your life. Life is a recurring cycle. It repeats itself. Embrace what you go through because you should be learning something everyday from everyone you encounter that you will need later in life to help you reach your destiny. You will encounter these scenarios again and again to test if you learned from before or not. Mental note: There is no easy way around this thing called life, so get ready. Life is a forever learning process.

Sixth, if I could tell my younger self something, I would say, "believe people when they show you who they are." You cannot change people nor should you want to. Do not ask someone to change. You don't ask people to change because forced decisions lead to deception. True change only occurs when someone voluntarily chooses to change because they realized they need to change. Not because someone said they need to change. They may be happy with who they are. You have three choices 1. Accept them for who they show you they are. 2. Properly categorize them in your life and make sure they know their title. 3. Do not allow them in your life at all. It is your personal choice to make.

Seventh, appreciate everything you are going through because it is either making you into a better or worse person: you get to choose. God does allow you freedom to choose who you want to become. Everything does works out for your good-it is not just a saying. Allow yourself to Trust the process. Pray and ask the Lord to remove anything that are not for you and only allow the things that are going to help you grow. I rebuke any negative thoughts or doubts that may be lingering around you today. In Jesus name, Amen.

Eighth, people say that money is the root to all evil. I must disagree. There are some good people who have a lot of money that bless others because they are blessed. Then there are others who make people feel bad because they do not have as much. Money can make good people better or bad people worse. The truth is the love of money and the lack of money is the root to all evil. Do not focus on having the most money, focus on having a relationship with God so that everything else will fall into place. Do not love the world or the things in the world. *"If anyone loves the world, the love of the father is not in them."* (Common English Bible, 1 John 2:15).

Prayer: You are a child of the highest God, he loves you, and He will never leave you, he has promised to prosper you. God has a purpose for your life. So, seek Him and He will find you. He is always with you; He just wants you to acknowledge his presence. With God all things are possible, when you are scared, mad, sad, happy, nervous, anxious, or hurt speak to Him. Even if you do not know what to say just call his name. Jesus! Thank you, Lord. Thank you for never leaving me, thank you for making me the head and not the tail. Thank you, Lord, for a sound mind and peaceful heart. I give you all the honor and praise in Jesus' name, Amen.

Proverbs 9

Invitations of Wisdom and Folly
1
Wisdom has built her house;
    she has set up[a] its seven pillars.
2
She has prepared her meat and mixed her wine;
    she has also set her table.
3
She has sent out her servants, and she calls
    from the highest point of the city,
4
    "Let all who are simple come to my house!"
To those who have no sense she says,
5
    "Come, eat my food
    and drink the wine I have mixed.
6
Leave your simple ways and you will live;
    walk in the way of insight."
7
Whoever corrects a mocker invites insults;
    whoever rebukes the wicked incurs abuse.
8
Do not rebuke mockers or they will hate you;
    rebuke the wise and they will love you.
9
Instruct the wise and they will be wiser still;
    teach the righteous and they will add to their learning.
10
The fear of the Lord is the beginning of wisdom,
    and knowledge of the Holy One is understanding.
11
For through wisdom[b] your days will be many,
    and years will be added to your life.

12

If you are wise, your wisdom will reward you;

    if you are a mocker, you alone will suffer.

13

Folly is an unruly woman;

    she is simple and knows nothing.

14

She sits at the door of her house,

    on a seat at the highest point of the city,

15

calling out to those who pass by,

    who go straight on their way,

16

    "Let all who are simple come to my house!"

To those who have no sense she says,

17

    "Stolen water is sweet;

    food eaten in secret is delicious!"

18

But little do they know that the dead are there,

    that her guests are deep in the realm of the dead.

CHAPTER 10

Take responsibility for your actions!

Every choice you will make has a consequence, it may be negative or positive. The result is based on your decision-making skills. When you make decisions based off your emotions or based off what you want to do. More than likely that is the wrong decision. Whatever you decide, own it. You should never make a permanent decision based on a temporary feeling. When you are mad, do not react. Do like I do: wait until tomorrow to respond. My thought process is after I have had time to think and clear my mind and weigh out my options. Especially when you are having a verbal argument. I can respond properly and not based off my initial emotion. Words last and they hurt. Your tongue is a powerful tool, use it to speak life into people and use it wisely. One bad decision can ruin your life or set you back from reaching God's plan for your life.

When you make the wrong choices, the wrong things will begin to follow. Whenever in doubt, cast all your concerns to the Lord and wait on your answer from Him. A good way to make decisions is to weigh your pros and cons of the situation. Whichever list has more you can lean more towards that decision, but then pray on it. Always pray and ask the Lord what you need from Him right then. The Lord will never leave you or forsake you, meaning He will always be there when you need Him. Even when you do not feel Him, just call on His name, Jesus. He promises He will always be with you even when you think He is not.

The best way is to pray is to start it off with the Lord's Prayer: Heavenly Father hallowed be thy name in kingdom come thy will be done on earth as it in in heaven give us this day our daily bread and forgive us our debts as we forgive our debtors and lead us not into temptation but deliver us from evil, for thine is the kingdom, and the power and the glory, forever and then thank the lord for all he has done in your life, what he has promised, what he will bring to past, then ask for discernment and guidance or whatever you need. Prayer works. Some prayers God answers quickly, some take time, but they are all answered right on time.

Seek God always to lead you when you are lost and when you are unsure of what decision to make. The Lord can speak to you through anything, someone close or a stranger, a radio broadcast, a voice, an unusual thought from how you normally think. God has no limits to how He will communicate to you. Pray and wait for His answer. Confirmation comes in 2's & 3's. There are no real coincidences. When you hear something over and over, you better listen. The things that are supposed to happen will happen as planned. God can only produce good. He promises that he will see you through a bad situation, not that you will not encounter bad situations.

Prayer: Thank you, Lord for hearing my cry and never failing me. You are an on-time God. In Jesus name, Amen.

NIVS, Proverbs 10

Proverbs of Solomon
    1 The proverbs of Solomon:
A wise son brings joy to his father,
    but a foolish son brings grief to his mother.
2
Ill-gotten treasures have no lasting value,
    but righteousness delivers from death.

3
The Lord does not let the righteous go hungry,
   but he thwarts the craving of the wicked.
4
Lazy hands make for poverty,
   but diligent hands bring wealth.
5 He who gathers crops in summer is a prudent son,
   but he who sleeps during harvest is a disgraceful son.
6
Blessings crown the head of the righteous,
   but violence overwhelms the mouth of the wicked.[a]
7
The name of the righteous is used in blessings,[b]
   but the name of the wicked will rot.
8
The wise in heart accept commands,
   but a chattering fool comes to ruin.
9
Whoever walks in integrity walks securely,
   but whoever takes crooked paths will be found out.
10
Whoever winks maliciously causes grief,
   and a chattering fool comes to ruin.
11
The mouth of the righteous is a fountain of life,
   but the mouth of the wicked conceals violence.
12
Hatred stirs up conflict,
   but love covers over all wrongs.
13
Wisdom is found on the lips of the discerning,
   but a rod is for the back of one who has no sense.
14 The wise store up knowledge,
   but the mouth of a fool invites ruin.

15
The wealth of the rich is their fortified city,
  but poverty is the ruin of the poor.
16
The wages of the righteous is life,
  but the earnings of the wicked are sin and death.
17
Whoever heeds discipline shows the way to life,
  but whoever ignores correction leads others astray.
18
Whoever conceals hatred with lying lips
  and spreads slander is a fool.
19
Sin is not ended by multiplying words,
  but the prudent hold their tongues.
20
The tongue of the righteous is choice silver,
  but the heart of the wicked is of little value.
21
The lips of the righteous nourish many,
  but fools die for lack of sense.
22
The blessing of the Lord brings wealth,
  without painful toil for it.
23
A fool finds pleasure in wicked schemes,
  but a person of understanding delights in wisdom.
24
What the wicked dread will overtake them;
  what the righteous desire will be granted.
25
When the storm has swept by, the wicked are gone,
  but the righteous stand firm forever.
26
As vinegar to the teeth and smoke to the eyes,
  so are sluggards to those who send them.

27

The fear of the Lord adds length to life,

    but the years of the wicked are cut short.

28

The prospect of the righteous is joy,

    but the hopes of the wicked come to nothing.

29

The way of the Lord is a refuge for the blameless,

    but it is the ruin of those who do evil.

30

The righteous will never be uprooted,

    but the wicked will not remain in the land.

31

From the mouth of the righteous comes the fruit of wisdom,

    but a perverse tongue will be silenced.

32

The lips of the righteous know what finds favor,

but the mouth of the wicked only what is perverse.

CHAPTER 11

Building Character

Your character is how people view you. If you lie, you're labeled as a liar, if you cheat, you are a cheater, if you're promiscuous (to nicely say it) you're labeled as what the old folks would say that little fast girl. Your character is created by how you carry yourself, how you act towards others, how you treat your teachers, how you treat your friends, how you dress, how you speak, do you respect authority, do you get good grades, do you gossip or do you keep your word? Be mindful of your actions because, based on your behavior, people will form an opinion about you. No one should judge you as a person but, they can judge your character, so you do not want to build a bad track record.

High school is the four most important years of your life as a teenager. When it comes to building your character, how you conduct yourself in high school is how people will remember you. Your character can be changed over time with prayer, obedience, and maturity. If you try to walk in the image and likeness of the Lord, nothing can be said about you but good things. I said "try" because all we can do daily is try. We will fall short of glory because we are human, but God gives us grace to try again every day. No one is perfect but God. Be aware of haters, baby girl, people will gossip whether you are smart, not so smart, cute, not so cute, plump, or skinny. That song sticks and stones will break my bones, but words would not hurt me: that is not true. Words hurt just as bad and worse they stick with you. Always remember: you are a child of the highest God and if you stay true to his word you will have trials, but you will go through them gracefully.

Build your character by seeking God's word. You will try to live this life the way you want to, but you will get tired of things not going the way you want them to go and you will surrender. Once you give your all to the Lord, you will start to receive what the Lord has in store for you. The goal of life is to walk in the likeness of Christ. As you go through life and overcome obstacles you will begin to build your true character and it will be revealed as the person you want to be known for. Then you will begin to act accordingly. There are ways the Lord expects us to be: These ways are called "the fruit of the spirit" which consist of love, joy, peace, patience, kindness, goodness, faithfulness, self-control, and gentleness towards others. To begin your walk with Christ you must begin to embrace these 8 qualities.

Prayer: Thank you, Lord, for helping me to build my character in a way it aligns with your plan for my life. Amen.

NIV, Proverbs 11

1 The Lord detests dishonest scales,
   but accurate weights find favor with him.
2
When pride comes, then comes disgrace,
   but with humility comes wisdom.
3
The integrity of the upright guides them,
   but the unfaithful are destroyed by their duplicity.
4
Wealth is worthless in the day of wrath,
   but righteousness delivers from death.
5
The righteousness of the blameless makes their paths straight,
   but the wicked are brought down by their own wickedness.

6
The righteousness of the upright delivers them,
    but the unfaithful are trapped by evil desires.
7
Hopes placed in mortals die with them;
    all the promise of[a] their power comes to nothing.
8
The righteous person is rescued from trouble,
    and it falls on the wicked instead.
9
With their mouths the godless destroy their neighbors,
    but through knowledge the righteous escape.
10
When the righteous prosper, the city rejoices;
    when the wicked perish, there are shouts of joy.
11
Through the blessing of the upright a city is exalted,
    but by the mouth of the wicked it is destroyed.
12
Whoever derides their neighbor has no sense,
    but the one who has understanding holds their tongue.
13
A gossip betrays a confidence,
    but a trustworthy person keeps a secret.
14
For lack of guidance a nation falls,
    but victory is won through many advisers.
15
Whoever puts up security for a stranger will surely suffer,
    but whoever refuses to shake hands in pledge is safe.
16
A kindhearted woman gains honor,
    but ruthless men gain only wealth.
17
Those who are kind benefit themselves,
    but the cruel bring ruin on themselves.

18

A wicked person earns deceptive wages,

    but the one who sows righteousness reaps a sure reward.

19

Truly the righteous attain life,

    but whoever pursues evil finds death.

20

The Lord detests those whose hearts are perverse,

    but he delights in those whose ways are blameless.

21

Be sure of this: The wicked will not go unpunished,

    but those who are righteous will go free.

22

Like a gold ring in a pig's snout

    is a beautiful woman who shows no discretion.

23

The desire of the righteous ends only in good,

    but the hope of the wicked only in wrath.

24

One person gives freely, yet gains even more;

    another withholds unduly, but comes to poverty.

25

A generous person will prosper;

    whoever refreshes others will be refreshed.

26

People curse the one who hoards grain,

    but they pray God's blessing on the one who is willing to sell.

27

Whoever seeks good finds favor,

    but evil comes to one who searches for it.

28

Those who trust in their riches will fall,

    but the righteous will thrive like a green leaf.

29

Whoever brings ruin on their family will inherit only wind,

    and the fool will be servant to the wise.

30

The fruit of the righteous is a tree of life,
  and the one who is wise saves lives.

31

If the righteous receive their due on earth,
  how much more the ungodly and the sinner!

CHAPTER 12

Continually try to live life the right way

Repeat x 3 I am a child of God and I will live life according to his word.

Regardless of your own emotional fulfillment and selfish desires. There is a right way to live your time here on earth. Such as being generous to people, the ones you know and have never seen before. Give help when you can, just because you can, and do not mistreat people. Be obedient to the word of God even when tempted. Becoming this person mentioned in these few sentences takes times, but as you try everyday it will become a part of the new person you chose to become and will then come naturally. No one is perfect but God, he gives you grace to try it again another day. Be selfless and think of others.

Love God first then yourself and don't allow anyone to treat you any ole' kind of way. Set boundaries to how you want to be treated. You can teach people how to treat you by not dealing with people who do not treat you the way you want to be treated. If someone does not treat you with respect, then do not associate with them. That is your personal choice. Respect people and expect to be respected. You do not have to be friends with anyone you do not want to if they do not respect you.

As a teenager, your focus should be to go to school, play team sports so you learn how to work as a team. Life is about building bonds and working with people: you will benefit by being on a team. Be a great person all the time. Love the Lord and pray continually, Thank the Lord daily, randomly for even the small blessings. You are who you are because the Lord made you specifically to be you. Be great in your own way. Get good grades, learn how to deal with people, be sociable, praise people for their accomplishments, and forgive people who hurt you. The Bible states, *"but be very careful to keep the commandment and the law that Moses the servant of the Lord gave you: to love the Lord your God, to walk in obedience to him, to keep his commands, to hold fast to him and to serve him with all your heart and with all your soul."* (NIV, Joshua 22:5)

God says to follow his commands:
The 10 commandments are:
Put God first.
Worship God only.
Use God's name with respect.
Remember God's sabbath
Respect your parents.
Do not hurt other people.
Be faithful in marriage.
Do not Steal.
Do not kill.
Do not want what others have.

This request is easier said than done. We live in the time where we have free will to do as we please. If you understand why you are here (your purpose), life will be so much better than you think. Being obedient verses doing what you think you want to. If you are hardheaded and start off on the wrong path, it is only a matter of time before you choose to follow the plan God has for your life. You can only deal with so much before you get sick and tired of being sick and tired. Everybody has a testimony, what will yours be? That is why we do not judge people, because no sin is worse than the next. All sin is bad.

Prayer: Thank you for allowing me to humble and be obedient to your word, so that I can live according to your will for my life. In Jesus' name, Amen.

NIV, Proverbs 12

1 Whoever loves discipline loves knowledge,
  but whoever hates correction is stupid.

2
Good people obtain favor from the Lord,
  but he condemns those who devise wicked schemes.

3
No one can be established through wickedness,
  but the righteous cannot be uprooted.

4
A wife of noble character is her husband's crown,
  but a disgraceful wife is like decay in his bones.

5
The plans of the righteous are just,
  but the advice of the wicked is deceitful.

6
The words of the wicked lie in wait for blood,
  but the speech of the upright rescues them.

7
The wicked are overthrown and are no more,
  but the house of the righteous stands firm.

8
A person is praised according to their prudence,
  and one with a warped mind is despised.

9
Better to be a nobody and yet have a servant
  than pretend to be somebody and have no food.

10
The righteous care for the needs of their animals,
  but the kindest acts of the wicked are cruel.

11

Those who work their land will have abundant food,
  but those who chase fantasies have no sense.

12

The wicked desire the stronghold of evildoers,
  but the root of the righteous endures.

13

Evildoers are trapped by their sinful talk,
  and so the innocent escape trouble.

14

From the fruit of their lips people are filled with good things,
  and the work of their hands brings them reward.

15

The way of fools seems right to them,
  but the wise listen to advice.

16 Fools show their annoyance at once,
  but the prudent overlook an insult.

17

An honest witness tells the truth,
  but a false witness tells lies.

18

The words of the reckless pierce like swords,
  but the tongue of the wise brings healing.

19

Truthful lips endure forever,
  but a lying tongue lasts only a moment.

20

Deceit is in the hearts of those who plot evil,
  but those who promote peace have joy.

21

No harm overtakes the righteous,
  but the wicked have their fill of trouble.

22

The Lord detests lying lips,
  but he delights in people who are trustworthy.

23

The prudent keep their knowledge to themselves,
  but a fool's heart blurts out folly.

24 Diligent hands will rule,
  but laziness ends in forced labor.

25

Anxiety weighs down the heart,
  but a kind word cheers it up.

26

The righteous choose their friends carefully,
  but the way of the wicked leads them astray.

27

The lazy do not roast[a] any game,
  but the diligent feed on the riches of the hunt.

28

In the way of righteousness there is life;
  along that path is immortality.

CHAPTER 13

Mamas Rules

Repeat x3 I am a child of God and I will obey my parents.

Nobody likes rules, but the reason parents have rules are to mold you and prepare you for the rules of the land. God has rules as well. So, you are never exempt from rules no matter what age. Mamas rules are not to stop you from enjoying your youth but to protect you and prepare for the real world. Think about it. If you grow up with no rules and no one to answer to, when you are older, you will have a mindset that you can do whatever you want. You will have a mentality that the rules do not apply to you because that's how you grew up, you will end up in a bad situation or worse, prison. Rules are what mold you as an individual. Rules and laws are what help the world run properly. If we had no stop lights, everybody would crash and run into each other all the time. Look what happens now when you disobey the signals. Just imagine if there were no lights at all. What if we did not have laws, no one would be safe to walk outside. So, respect rules they are to protect us all.

You must follow rules as an adult as well as when you are a child. A different set but still rules. My stepdad told my oldest daughter, when she was 14 years old, "You will be an adult for way longer than you will be a child so enjoy your fun of not paying bills and getting up going to work. Enjoy being taken care of because trust and believe you will say at least once, when you are older. "I wish I was a kid again, with no responsibilities because I'm tired of paying bills." Enjoy the privilege of being taken care of and know your only responsibility is to be respectful and obey your parents.

Now, my daughter who is 19 yrs old said recently, "Oh my gosh, I am so tired of working and when I get my check the money is already gone!" I looked at her and said, "you are the one who wanted your own phone bill and a car note. Don't be mad now, you got what you wanted." We always think we want something until we get it and it's like oh naw, I didn't mean like that. Hopefully, your parents are teaching you how to be an adult by actions but, if not, you know in your heart what is right and what is wrong. When having to choose what is right, base it off humility (putting others first by giving up what you think you deserve). Answer these questions, Am I doing this to please me? Will I hurt someone in the process? Remember: one bad decision is all it takes to ruin your life.

Prayer: Thank you, Lord, for a sound mind, please help me to make the best decision in this situation and state the situation. In Jesus name. Amen.

NIV, Proverbs 13

1
A wise son heeds his father's instruction,
 but a mocker does not respond to rebukes.
2
From the fruit of their lips people enjoy good things,
 but the unfaithful have an appetite for violence.
3
Those who guard their lips preserve their lives,
 but those who speak rashly will come to ruin.
4
A sluggard's appetite is never filled,
 but the desires of the diligent are fully satisfied.

5

The righteous hate what is false,
    but the wicked make themselves a stench
    and bring shame on themselves.

6

Righteousness guards the person of integrity,
    but wickedness overthrows the sinner.

7

One person pretends to be rich, yet has nothing;
    another pretends to be poor, yet has great wealth.

8

A person's riches may ransom their life,
    but the poor cannot respond to threatening rebukes.

9

The light of the righteous shines brightly,
    but the lamp of the wicked is snuffed out.

10

Where there is strife, there is pride,
    but wisdom is found in those who take advice.

11

Dishonest money dwindles away,
    but whoever gathers money little by little makes it grow.

12

Hope deferred makes the heart sick,
    but a longing fulfilled is a tree of life.

13

Whoever scorns instruction will pay for it,
    but whoever respects a command is rewarded.

14

The teaching of the wise is a fountain of life,
    turning a person from the snares of death.

15

Good judgment wins favor,
    but the way of the unfaithful leads to their destruction.[a]

16

All who are prudent act with[b] knowledge,

    but fools expose their folly.

17

A wicked messenger falls into trouble,

    but a trustworthy envoy brings healing.

18

Whoever disregards discipline comes to poverty and shame,

    but whoever heeds correction is honored.

19

A longing fulfilled is sweet to the soul,

    but fools detest turning from evil.

20

Walk with the wise and become wise,

    for a companion of fools suffers harm.

21

Trouble pursues the sinner,

    but the righteous are rewarded with good things.

22

A good person leaves an inheritance for their children's children,

    but a sinner's wealth is stored up for the righteous.

23 An unplowed field produces food for the poor,

    but injustice sweeps it away.

24 Whoever spares the rod hates their children,

    but the one who loves their children is careful to discipline them.

25 The righteous eat to their hearts' content,

    but the stomach of the wicked goes hungry.

CHAPTER 14

A Father's message for his daughter!!

Repeat: I also have a father in heaven who loves me!

A father's love is the missing piece in the hearts of all little girls who grow up without him. No matter how strong you may seem or may think, you don't need your dad nothing, but God can replace that hole that's in your heart where he belongs. Baby girl stop looking for validation and value from some random man. The only man you need is your Father in Heaven. He is your provider, protector, healer, way maker, light in the darkness, he is the only man that will never leave you. He is your everything. I promise you will not find what you are looking for to complete you in any man, but Jesus.

Some of us aren't as fortunate to grow up with our biological fathers and those of us who don't, we have a hole in our hearts where that father's love is missing. So, we tend to try to fill it with any type of attention, good or bad because we are feening for something that we never had but we are blindly seeking it. Unfortunately, you do not realize it until later in life, when you have been repeatedly broken and mistreated by boys/men who you think will fill that hole but end up taking advantage of the situation.

Most females go through life searching for something or someone to complete them or make them feel whole. It could literally be 20 years of dating the wrong guys or the same type of guys who use and abuse you, mentally, emotionally, physically, sexually, or financially until they make you feel like you do not deserve better. Baby girl, you are a princess on your way to becoming a Queen, Do Not believe that you don't deserve the best. Psalm 139 :13-14 NIV says "you are the one who put me together inside my mother's body, and I praise you because of the wonderful way you created me. Everything you do is marvelous! Of this, I have no doubt." The Lord is telling you he created you in his perfection, nothing about you is flawed, he created you perfectly to the point he knows every hair on your head. Love the Lord with all your heart because He loves you.

I cannot tell you what a father would say to his daughter. So, I had some of my male friends including my daughters' father, who I believe are great fathers write up some messages. This is what I asked them: Being that you were a boy once upon a time, knowing how boys think about girls during these teenage years with all your raging hormones and peer pressure, what would you tell or have already told your daughters regarding life, love, school, or boys?

"I would tell her to just focus on school and leave these boys alone; it's a distraction." ~ J. Burgess

"Trust in the Lord." ~D. Hawkins

"I will tell my daughter to respect herself at all times, don't let nobody use you or make you feel like you're worth nothing. Focus on your schoolwork so you can go to college or a trade school or anything that's going to make you successful. Before you get in any relationship make sure you love yourself before you claim to love somebody else. Only when you love yourself you will find that person that loves you just as much as you love yourself. Don't let a man peer pressure you into having sex. Wait until you're ready. When you're ready make sure you protect yourself at all cost, no matter what the person says everything is on your time if they cannot respect that they're not the one for you. Establish yourself before you build a family because it's a lot harder trying to build something for yourself when you have kids so make sure you have everything in order before you take that next step in life. This is the most important thing never give up on yourself and never give up on life no matter how hard it is never quit once you quit it's going to take a long time for you to get yourself back together so keep fighting." ~A. Amason

"Honestly, all I tell my daughters is the most important relationship to have is with God, and everything else will fall in place. Our relationship with God is meant to be cryptic and personal, but in it, He tells us when, where, how, who, and to what extent. So, I would tell a teenager to not worry about what his or her friends are doing, although those relationships are important, but not as important as the one you have with God. A weak mind allows others to define them, free thought is one of the greatest gifts God gave us, so collective thought, to me, is a slap in the face of God." ~ I. Henderson

"I taught mine that if you don't focus on love you won't get hurt or blinded by it. Most people don't understand what it is, but always get what it does to the mind. Boys will be there long after the journey of them getting their life together. Know that you are Queens." ~ D. Bryant

"To my daughters. Life is about you. Not your relationship with guys. No one cares about you more than you. You come first. To reassure that, prioritize your wants and goals. They both should revolve around your dreams. As a teen you are going to experience a lot of different emotions and get tested by boys. Again, focus on you. Separate what you want from what you need. You need to be financially independent. That is your main responsibility, if not only. Boys and relationships are going to come down the line. But are you happy with yourself is key? Don't hesitate to make a decision that is going to benefit you. Money doesn't make itself and please don't depend on anyone to give you money or make money for you. Don't degrade yourself for money. Educate yourself for money. I want to see you grow up to be a respectable, responsible independent woman. Life will be unfair. Just smile and work smarter to make sure you are getting your share. And always share. Your big smile and beautiful heart goes a long way in the eyes of your supporter." ~ D. Combo

"Dear baby girl,

How are you? I'm writing you to inform you on love, sex, boys, and life from a man's point of view. I've been alive for 36 years now and have encountered thousands of boys, girls, men, and women. I'm just going to give you a perspective from what I've encountered.

Boys,

As a father of girls, I have a different outlook on females. I was a boy at one point in time too though. I used to be immature and I didn't know what was special about a girl, All I knew was that they were different from me. I had some female friends that were fun to chill and hang around but as I got older, I began to feel a different type of emotional liking to females. Not knowing or understanding what I was feeling I just went with the flow. Boys are simple at a young age. They are easily influenced by their friends and haven't developed their own identity yet. Once he gets to middle school, he begins to search for himself and try to figure out who he is and what he wants in life. So, baby girl love from a boy at this age is almost impossible, so don't try to get involved. They are still learning to love themselves. It's also the beginning of him learning how his body works and if he is even interested in getting involved with a female in a relationship type of level. At this age they are trying to understand the difference between life and if they like the female as a friend or girlfriend. Most of the time they are influenced by older siblings or friends. As time passes, they begin to develop into who they want to be. Majority of them start to want sex because this is what they think will make the man amongst their friends. Whoever can have sex with the most girls is considered cool or big dawg. Their way of thinking is molded by and of what they've seen by others, TV, and music. So, they don't know how to respect women, only their mother and sometimes not even her. A lot of boys are still innocent and green(lame) to some girls but the transition from eighth grade to high school is a big jump. The boy feels that he is a man now and getting the girls for the goodies is what he's focused on. But being a ninth grader, they are considered the babies of high school so they really don't get a lot of play, but when they get a 10th grade, they kind of boss up a little bit and develop their own identity of the man that he will become. He will begin to learn to love he may also learn to hate love if he experiences heartbreak. Peer pressure is real and dangerous. All through the rest of high school 11th and 12th grade are the cool years, because they feel like men. They are the big dogs now and many of them have ideas about what they want to do after high school and what their friends think of them means a lot. After high school they regress cause the freedom of high school allows him to let it all hang out. A lot of them will mess up their lives during the summer after high school. Those are the years that boys need the most guidance. Once he's out of high school the sky's the limit. He must find ways to survive for the rest of his life. So, he must figure out if he is going to make money the right way and get an honest job or fall victim to the streets, some stay bums but with money comes temptation, mainly girls. They come from every everywhere throwing sex at him left and right. He doesn't understand it all but all he can think about is having sex with the girl not thinking of the later consequences. This is also the time when a lot of dudes are introduced to hard drugs. They first got introduced to it in high school but now they are amongst adults and they are younger they are easily influenced. He is willing to experience the club, parties, and drug life. Most of the time men are introduced to hard drugs by females around 18-26 years old. So, from that age frame it is hard to get a decent guy. Age 27 and up he begins to change his way of thinking because he has a family now and a family becomes a priority. Not all men get it, some men no matter how old they get, will never become a man, he will forever be a grown boy. It took a lot of trials and mistakes to find the man in me. As a father of two daughters, I learned that I want to treat my wife the way I would want a man to treat my girls.

Love,

As far as love goes, when you finally fall in love it can be the best thing you will ever encounter or could be the worst. Love has different feelings. There is the love you have for your family, then there is the feeling of being in love. When you are in love with someone you have selfless loyalty to that person. Love is like a duty and it's your duty to cherish the heart of your partner and do what you have to do to please and make your partner happy. True love is not always easy. Love can be a challenge but no matter what the power of love will prevail.

Sex,

Sex is something natural but also something that should be valued. As a 36-year-old man this is my position on this subject. I feel in women they should view sex as a gift from God, a part of them that should be protected and cherished until marriage. A part of them that should be earned by a man. A female should value herself. Because you have a boyfriend or a guy that you like who wants you, doesn't mean he gets or has to explore your body. Your virginity should be your pride and should be treated as such. Nowadays a lot of females are confused about sex and use it as a tool to get with they want, instead of using it to express their Love and loyalty to their partner. The generations today have no respect for themselves and see having sex is looked at as fun. Most females don't develop value for themselves until they have matured, go through trial and error with a few bad dudes who they thought liked them but used them for sex, and realized how they should value themselves. Like everything else, music influences us to think that's how life is supposed to be. It gets displayed as something you do for fun and pleasure instead of an emotional practice between two people to express their love for one another than just a physical encounter.

Life,

Life is short and it'll pass you by if you're not careful. Life is intended for us to live righteously and the way that the Lord wants us to live and worship him. We are born and raised by our parents who teach us how to live and survive. As we get older, things our parents didn't or couldn't teach us we learn from our own experiences in our lives we then pass our knowledge of those experiences to our kids to prepare them for life and all our generations to come. Life is about love, loyalty, fun and being obedient to god." ~F.Douglas

Prayer: Thank you, Lord for the good men you created, who are inspired to help your daughters through these difficult times. I pray that these words touch the hearts of many. In Jesus name, Amen.

NIV,Proverbs 14

1The wise woman builds her house,
    but with her own hands the foolish one tears hers down.
2
Whoever fears the Lord walks uprightly,
    but those who despise him are devious in their ways.
3
A fool's mouth lashes out with pride,
    but the lips of the wise protect them.
4
Where there are no oxen, the manger is empty,
    but from the strength of an ox come abundant harvests.
5
An honest witness does not deceive,
    but a false witness pours out lies.
6
The mocker seeks wisdom and finds none,
    but knowledge comes easily to the discerning.
7
Stay away from a fool,
    for you will not find knowledge on their lips.
8
The wisdom of the prudent is to give thought to their ways,
    but the folly of fools is deception.
9
Fools mock at making amends for sin,
    but goodwill is found among the upright.
10
Each heart knows its own bitterness,
    and no one else can share its joy.
11
The house of the wicked will be destroyed,
    but the tent of the upright will flourish.

12
There is a way that appears to be right,
  but in the end it leads to death.

13
Even in laughter the heart may ache,
  and rejoicing may end in grief.

14
The faithless will be fully repaid for their ways,
  and the good rewarded for theirs.

15
The simple believe anything,
  but the prudent give thought to their steps.

16
The wise fear the Lord and shun evil,
  but a fool is hotheaded and yet feels secure.

17
A quick-tempered person does foolish things,
  and the one who devises evil schemes is hated.

18
The simple inherit folly,
  but the prudent are crowned with knowledge.

19
Evildoers will bow down in the presence of the good,
  and the wicked at the gates of the righteous.

20
The poor are shunned even by their neighbors,
  but the rich have many friends.

21
It is a sin to despise one's neighbor,
  but blessed is the one who is kind to the needy.

22
Do not those who plot evil go astray?
  But those who plan what is good find[a] love and faithfulness.

23
All hard work brings a profit,
  but mere talk leads only to poverty.

24
The wealth of the wise is their crown,
    but the folly of fools yields folly.

25
A truthful witness saves lives,
    but a false witness is deceitful.

26
Whoever fears the Lord has a secure fortress,
    and for their children it will be a refuge.

27
The fear of the Lord is a fountain of life,
    turning a person from the snares of death.

28
A large population is a king's glory,
    but without subjects a prince is ruined.

29
Whoever is patient has great understanding,
    but one who is quick-tempered displays folly.

30
A heart at peace gives life to the body,
    but envy rots the bones.

31
Whoever oppresses the poor shows contempt for their Maker,
    but whoever is kind to the needy honors God.

32
When calamity comes, the wicked are brought down,
    but even in death the righteous seek refuge in God.

33
Wisdom reposes in the heart of the discerning
    and even among fools she lets herself be known.[b]

34
Righteousness exalts a nation,
    but sin condemns any people.

35
A king delights in a wise servant,
    but a shameful servant arouses his fury.

Love Others

CHAPTER 15

Communication is Key!

We all learn to talk as toddlers and most of us know how to say what we want but do we really listen? True communication is when you and someone else are talking, either to get a point across, for leisure, motivation, or constructive criticism. To be able to communicate effectively is to be able to listen to what someone is saying fully before you start forming your response in your head. This shows you care about what is being said. Remember: people will not listen to you until they know you care. When you communicate, you cannot fully focus on what is being said if you are thinking of questions to ask while the other person is expressing their feelings or thoughts. Listen attentively and formulate any responses that you may have regarding what was said when they have finished. Express yourself by speaking what's on your mind. Honesty is always good but how to deliver the honesty may take asking God in prayer. Communication is the key to making any relationship work. Learn that your way isn't the only way. People have different perspectives when it comes to life. Respect their point of view, it will give you a better understanding of how they think for future conversations.

Remember: you speak life and death with the power of the tongue so be cautious of what you say. Once something is spoken you can be sorry for saying it, but you can never take it back, it was still said. So be kind, only speak positive things and think before you speak. Your words become reality, so only talk about what you want, not what you don't want. Speak good things over your life because you want good things to happen. When you go throughout your day communicate with the Lord, ask Him about the things He would like for you to accomplish. If it be His will it will be done. Think positive thoughts regardless of the situation. You will produce positive actions and positive things will follow.

God hears every cry out to Him. Build a relationship with the Lord by communicating with Him daily. A quick "thank you Jesus," will do if you have nothing else to say. Just acknowledge that you know He is there. Praise the Lord for all the bad and good things you are blessed to have, a house, a car, food to eat, toys to play with, a sound mind, to be able to communicate, your family, friends, both legs, both arms, their ability to work and most of all the breath in your body. There are people praying for at least one or more of those things they do not have. Speak the words of your heart and be thankful for all that you have.

Prayer: Thank you, Lord for blessing me with the ability to speak to you, guide my words so they can speak life to someone in need. Thank you, Father, for allowing me another day to try again. In Jesus' name, Amen.

Proverbs 15

1 A gentle answer turns away wrath,
    but a harsh word stirs up anger.
2
The tongue of the wise adorns knowledge,
    but the mouth of the fool gushes folly.
3
The eyes of the Lord are everywhere,
    keeping watch on the wicked and the good.
4
The soothing tongue is a tree of life,
    but a perverse tongue crushes the spirit.

5
A fool spurns a parent's discipline,
    but whoever heeds correction shows prudence.
6
The house of the righteous contains great treasure,
    but the income of the wicked brings ruin.
7
The lips of the wise spread knowledge,
    but the hearts of fools are not upright.
8
The Lord detests the sacrifice of the wicked,
    but the prayer of the upright pleases him.
9
The Lord detests the way of the wicked,
    but he loves those who pursue righteousness.
10
Stern discipline awaits anyone who leaves the path;
    the one who hates correction will die.
11
Death and Destruction[a] lie open before the Lord—
    how much more do human hearts!
12
Mockers resent correction,
    so they avoid the wise.
13
A happy heart makes the face cheerful,
    but heartache crushes the spirit.
14
The discerning heart seeks knowledge,
    but the mouth of a fool feeds on folly.
15
All the days of the oppressed are wretched,
    but the cheerful heart has a continual feast.
16
Better a little with the fear of the Lord
    than great wealth with turmoil.

17
Better a small serving of vegetables with love
     than a fattened calf with hatred.
18
A hot-tempered person stirs up conflict,
     but the one who is patient calms a quarrel.
19
The way of the sluggard is blocked with thorns,
     but the path of the upright is a highway.
20
A wise son brings joy to his father,
     but a foolish man despises his mother.
21
Folly brings joy to one who has no sense,
     but whoever has understanding keeps a straight course.
22
Plans fail for lack of counsel,
     but with many advisers they succeed.
23
A person finds joy in giving an apt reply—
     andhowgoodisatimelywordH+–33Ho+–ia3306
24
The path of life leads upward for the prudent
     to keep them from going down to the realm of the dead.
25
The Lord tears down the house of the proud,
     but he sets the widow's boundary stones in place.
26
The Lord detests the thoughts of the wicked,
     but gracious words are pure in his sight.
27
The greedy bring ruin to their households,
     but the one who hates bribes will live.
28
The heart of the righteous weighs its answers,
     but the mouth of the wicked gushes evil.

29

The Lord is far from the wicked,
   but he hears the prayer of the righteous.

30

Light in a messenger's eyes brings joy to the heart,
   and good news gives health to the bones.

31

Whoever heeds life-giving correction
   will be at home among the wise.

32

Those who disregard discipline despise themselves,
   but the one who heeds correction gains understanding.

33

Wisdom's instruction is to fear the Lord,
   and humility comes before honor.

CHAPTER 16

Toxic Relationships

Toxic relationships are relationships that are not beneficial for your well-being. An example of a toxic relationship can be categorized in a range of negative behaviors from constant arguing, jealousy, controlling, self-seeking behavior, verbal, physical, or mental abuse. Arguing stems from the inability to see things from the other person's perspective. It is not necessary to try to agree with what the other person is saying but to understand how they feel or what they mean is the goal. An agreement to disagree is always the solution. Remember you are all separate people trying to come together as friends or couples so there might always be misunderstandings. Communicate effectively so that your point is expressed, and you receive the other person's point of view.

Strongholds / Soul ties are real. Strongholds and soul ties are interchangeable. They are like addictions to a certain person mainly through sex. Soul ties keep you trapped in situations that are no good for you. Strongholds are from the devil. The only way to break a stronghold is to pray and ask for it to be broken and for you to be released. Strongholds have the power to make you believe you can't leave and that you don't deserve better. This is the farthest from the truth, our Father says "For I know the plans I have for you. Plans to prosper you and not to harm you, plans to give you hope and a future." Jeremiah 29:11

Do not allow fear to enter your heart. Fear is not from above but from below. So, rebuke that fear demon in the name of Jesus. When breaking strongholds, it's a part of life to grow apart from people, so understand that everybody is not meant to go through your journey with you. Some people in your life may be toxic even if they don't display those toxic signs. Everybody that is in your life isn't for you. Some people come for seasons. Don't allow someone who was supposed to pitch a tent build a home in your heart. There are some people you may think are your friends who prey on your weaknesses or wish bad on your life. This may even be someone close to you.

I like to describe this situation as being inside a box. Everyone outside the box can see what is really going on but, you cannot because you are inside the box. So, things will seem different to you, but once you notice what is happening that is just the beginning. *It will take a lot of prayer, strength that only the lord can provide and time to be ready to leave a toxic relationship.* As crazy as it sounds, it will take time to leave a toxic relationship. It really does. You will probably think; "I would never stay somewhere I am being mistreated." Honey let me tell you. I said that too. Until I found myself being verbally abused, wondering "why am I still here?" I would leave and come back, this went on for years until I realized he is not going to change and if I wanted to change my situation, I had to change how I responded. If you want something different, you must do something different. It takes time to build confidence and end this revolving cycle.

Women often give chances even when chances are not deserved or earned. We give benefit of the doubt when it should not be given. We often stay in relationships longer than we should. The only positive outcome of staying is during this time you are building up that "sick and tired of being sick and tired" mentality that is needed to leave for real which will eventually be the reason you leave. Everybody has their own amount of drama they can accept so don't ever feel like you're not getting there, because you are. It is a process. These relationships can be avoided if you realize it in the beginning before you get too deep. But I think it takes for you to get deep before you realize what it is.

These relationships are emotionally draining and ruin it for when you are supposed to date Mr. Right. Be observant and notice the red flags. How are their relationships with other people? Do they seem to enjoy yelling and arguing, are they possessive, do they lack trust, are they verbally, mentally, or physically abusive, do they get jealous, or are they manipulative? These are some of the actions to ABORT MISSION QUICKLY when you start to see these signs. It doesn't take long to get to know a person's character if you pay attention. This is when your private investigative skills are needed. Take this needed time and put your feelings on the back burner to avoid getting them hurt. Sex during the getting to know each other phase, really messes it up, it puts blinders over all the red flags and all you can see is kissy faces and butterflies.

Dr. Robert Watkins says: DO NOT STAY ANYWHERE YOU DON'T FEEL VALUED!!

Prayer: Lord, help me to see who is for me and who is not before I enter into a toxic relationship. Protect me if I am in one and help me to build strength to remove myself. In Jesus' name, Amen.

Proverbs 16

1 To humans belong the plans of the heart,
    but from the Lord comes the proper answer of the tongue.
2
All a person's ways seem pure to them,
    but motives are weighed by the Lord.
3
Commit to the Lord whatever you do,
    and he will establish your plans.
4
The Lord works out everything to its proper end—
    even the wicked for a day of disaster.
5
The Lord detests all the proud of heart.
    Be sure of this: They will not go unpunished.

6

Through love and faithfulness sin is atoned for;
  through the fear of the Lord evil is avoided.

7

When the Lord takes pleasure in anyone's way,
  he causes their enemies to make peace with them.

8

Better a little with righteousness
  than much gain with injustice.

9

In their hearts humans plan their course,
  but the Lord establishes their steps.

10

The lips of a king speak as an oracle,
  and his mouth does not betray justice.

11

Honest scales and balances belong to the Lord;
  all the weights in the bag are of his making.

12

Kings detest wrongdoing,
  for a throne is established through righteousness.

13

Kings take pleasure in honest lips;
  they value the one who speaks what is right.

14

A king's wrath is a messenger of death,
  but the wise will appease it.

15

When a king's face brightens, it means life;
  his favor is like a rain cloud in spring.

16

How much better to get wisdom than gold,
  to get insight rather than silver!

17

The highway of the upright avoids evil;
  those who guard their ways preserve their lives.

18
Pride goes before destruction,
    a haughty spirit before a fall.
19
Better to be lowly in spirit along with the oppressed
    than to share plunder with the proud.
20
Whoever gives heed to instruction prospers,[a]
    and blessed is the one who trusts in the Lord.
21
The wise in heart are called discerning,
    and gracious words promote instruction.[b]
22
Prudence is a fountain of life to the prudent,
    but folly brings punishment to fools.
23
The hearts of the wise make their mouths prudent,
    and their lips promote instruction.[c]
24
Gracious words are a honeycomb,
    sweet to the soul and healing to the bones.
25
There is a way that appears to be right,
    but in the end it leads to death.
26
The appetite of laborers works for them;
    their hunger drives them on.
27 A scoundrel plots evil,
    and on their lips it is like a scorching fire.
28
A perverse person stirs up conflict,
    and a gossip separates close friends.
29
A violent person entices their neighbor
    and leads them down a path that is not good.

30

Whoever winks with their eye is plotting perversity;
  whoever purses their lips is bent on evil.

31

Gray hair is a crown of splendor;
  it is attained in the way of righteousness.

32

Better a patient person than a warrior,
  one with self-control than one who takes a city.

33

The lot is cast into the lap, but its every decision is from the Lord.

CHAPTER 17

How to let go of a toxic relationship!!

Ok, so this is like common sense but how many of you know common sense is not so common anymore? This is an issue that is the hardest for most females to do. It is a process. Knowing within your heart you are ready to leave and let go is the first step. Building the strength and confidence is the next step. Being able to commit and follow through with your decision to let go is the third step. Then putting the action that is needed to complete the mission is the fourth step. You can not be friends. It is impossible to be friends with someone you have had an emotional relationship with right after it's over and the breakup is not a mutual understanding where you agree a relationship isn't the best for either of you, or there are no hard or hurt feelings.

This is a tricky topic. Some of you do not get physically attached and are mentally strong to the point where you can just stop talking to someone. Mentally strong meaning, at the first sign of dishonesty you leave the relationship, with no hesitation at all. You can block their number and never hear from them again. Then there are some of you who must be all the way fed up with repeatedly being disrespected before you leave a situation. We tend to see the potential verses what he is showing us. Again, believe them when they show you who they are. If they did something once, they will likely do it again especially during high school years.

How do you let them go you ask? To let someone go, first your heart and your thoughts must be aligned. You cannot be torn inside to successfully let go. You must commit to a decision to move forward in the process and know that even if you feel weak, remember the mission. This is where prayer is needed to ask for strength, if you're about to give in, stand tall and remember all the reasons you are removing the person and ask "does the bad outweigh the good!" If it does, then you need to follow through with the exit. Remember your worth is valuable. Whoever you encounter should treat you as such or they don't deserve you.

Once your heart and mind are on the same page, to let someone go you must physically remove them from your everyday life. Do not answer texts, calls, direct messages, indirect posts on social media and do not try to get in contact with them at all. Avoid going places you know they will be. Distance yourself from mutual friends who may relay messages or bring them up. Your major focus during this time should be on healing and restoration of emotional strength. If you have kids together, you will need to keep the conversation to a minimal. Example: "Hi, I will be back at 9pm to get him/her." No small talk. No "just wanted to see how you are doing." Nothing. Short, sweet and to the point. Keep the convos to what needs to be communicated and that is it. When someone loses accessibility to you, your value becomes clearer. This will not be easy. Trust God. He will see you through.

If you know you get weak around the person or when you hear their rebuttal, then don't put yourself in that situation to allow your weakness to take over. Cut all communication with the person. It may take years to fully let go. Patience, consistency, and perseverance is key. "The Lord is my strength and my defense; he has become my salvation. He is my God, and I will praise him, my father's God, and I will exalt him." Exodus 15:2. New International Version

Prayer: Thank you for giving me the strength to endure the emotional pain from letting go of people who are not for me. In Jesus name, Amen.

Proverbs 17

1 Better a dry crust with peace and quiet
   than a house full of feasting, with strife.

2

A prudent servant will rule over a disgraceful son
   and will share the inheritance as one of the family.

3

The crucible for silver and the furnace for gold,
   but the Lord tests the heart.

4

A wicked person listens to deceitful lips;
   a liar pays attention to a destructive tongue.

5

Whoever mocks the poor shows contempt for their Maker;
   whoever gloats over disaster will not go unpunished.

6

Children's children are a crown to the aged,
   and parents are the pride of their children.

7

Eloquent lips are unsuited to a godless fool—
   how much worse lying lips to a ruler!

8

A bribe is seen as a charm by the one who gives it;
   they think success will come at every turn.

9

Whoever would foster love covers over an offense,
   but whoever repeats the matter separates close friends.

10

A rebuke impresses a discerning person
   more than a hundred lashes a fool.

11

Evildoers foster rebellion against God;
   the messenger of death will be sent against them.

12
Better to meet a bear robbed of her cubs
  than a fool bent on folly.
13
Evil will never leave the house
  of one who pays back evil for good.
14
Starting a quarrel is like breaching a dam;
  so drop the matter before a dispute breaks out.
15
Acquitting the guilty and condemning the innocent—
  the Lord detests them both.
16
Why should fools have money in hand to buy wisdom,
  when they are not able to understand it?
17
A friend loves at all times,
  and a brother is born for a time of adversity.
18
One who has no sense shakes hands in pledge
  and puts up security for a neighbor.
19
Whoever loves a quarrel loves sin;
  whoever builds a high gate invites destruction.
20
One whose heart is corrupt does not prosper;
  one whose tongue is perverse falls into trouble.
21 To have a fool for a child brings grief;
  there is no joy for the parent of a godless fool.
22
A cheerful heart is good medicine,
  but a crushed spirit dries up the bones.
23
The wicked accept bribes in secret
  to pervert the course of justice.

24
A discerning person keeps wisdom in view,
    but a fool's eyes wander to the ends of the earth.
25 A foolish son brings grief to his father
    and bitterness to the mother who bore him.
26
If imposing a fine on the innocent is not good,
    surely to flog honest officials is not right.
27
The one who has knowledge uses words with restraint,
    and whoever has understanding is even-tempered.
28
Even fools are thought wise if they keep silent,
    and discerning if they hold their tongues.

CHAPTER 18

Social Media and Reality TV

ocial media and reality TV are one in the same. They are both for entertainment purposes. How many hours do you catch yourself scrolling through everybody else's life or videos of people doing stupid things? They are either getting paid or trying to get paid to keep you watching. It's not real; the way they look, dress, act- they are always camera ready. You do not catch them waking up with the morning breath or crust in their eyes. They are always camera-ready, waiting for the drama to walk into the next scene. So, do not think you are supposed to live up to those individuals' standards. Everyone who indulges in those kinds of shows are not only trying to live as the people of the world but they live to please the people of the world. Social media is corrupting the minds of the children at a young age. So, just imagine the teenager's minds. Social media has made it appear to be ok to say what you want to say behind a computer and not suffer any consequences, just pierce the souls of people. People can say some hurtful things just because that's how they were feeling at that time. Social media is also trying to make everyone believe things that are not acceptable are now acceptable.

That is not the way the Lord wanted it to be. The Bible is an acronym that stands for "Basic Instructions Before Leaving Earth." The way we are supposed to live is in the Bible. Not based on how the reality stars are living. Have you ever seen an episode in which they attend church? Or pray together as a family? Or even thank the Lord for their meal.

Even if they do those things, they chose not to show them on TV. The only time you see the church is funerals or weddings. They don't want to bring us closer to God but direct your focus to worship the things they have or things they promote. Example: how many girls on social media has their body transformed because everybody on TV has a "bought body?" I remember when the shows that came on TV were constructive. They taught life lessons. Shows like Family Matters, The Cosby's, Living Single, Full House, The Golden Girls & even Martin. Colossians 3:5 (New International Version) says "put to death, therefore whatever your earthly nature: sexual immorality, impurity, lust, evil desires, and greed, which is idolatry." They are living this reckless life and then through there influential ability are making it seem ok to live this way.

Reality TV is not even real anymore, everything is just a distraction to keep us all from our purpose and full of sin. It has no morals behind it like the shows did back in the day. Oh My Gosh, I sound like my grandma. The older shows showed a family structure, examples of how you should be as a child, and what happened when you messed up. TV has changed over the years. It's not teaching anymore. Now you turn on the TV or phone, tablet and it's about whose fake body is better, whose weave is longer or better quality, whose clothes are more expensive and teaches nothing about life, morals, respect for yourself as a young lady. It doesn't tell you how to stay a virgin for your husband or how not to disfigure God's temple (your body). Now, everybody wants to look like and be like these reality TV stars. Everybody is doing any and everything to become famous, instead of focusing on real life and what is ahead of us. None of this will matter once your time expires. The Lord is not worried about how many followers you have but were you a follower and doer of His word. He will not reward you based on how many likes your "butt" shot received. The Lord is seeking your soul and is checking if you are walking in the image and likeness of Him. Are you?

Prayer: Lord, help me to be more like you, despite what I see in the world. In Jesus' name Amen.

Proverbs 18

1 An unfriendly person pursues selfish ends
  and against all sound judgment starts quarrels.

2
Fools find no pleasure in understanding
  but delight in airing their own opinions.

3
When wickedness comes, so does contempt,
  and with shame comes reproach.

4
The words of the mouth are deep waters,
  but the fountain of wisdom is a rushing stream.

5
It is not good to be partial to the wicked
  and so deprive the innocent of justice.

6
The lips of fools bring them strife,
  and their mouths invite a beating.

7
The mouths of fools are their undoing,
  and their lips are a snare to their very lives.

8
The words of a gossip are like choice morsels;
  they go down to the inmost parts.

9 One who is slack in his work
  is brother to one who destroys.

10
The name of the Lord is a fortified tower;
  therighteousruntoitandaresafe

11
The wealth of the rich is their fortified city;
  they imagine it a wall too high to scale.

12
Before a downfall the heart is haughty,
  but humility comes before honor.

13
To answer before listening—
　　that is folly and shame.
14
The human spirit can endure in sickness,
　　but a crushed spirit who can bear?
15
The heart of the discerning acquires knowledge,
　　for the ears of the wise seek it out.
16
A gift opens the way
　　and ushers the giver into the presence of the great.
17 In a lawsuit the first to speak seems right,
　　until someone comes forward and cross-examines.
18
Casting the lot settles disputes
　　and keeps strong opponents apart.
19
A brother wronged is more unyielding than a fortified city;
　　disputes are like the barred gates of a citadel.
20
From the fruit of their mouth a person's stomach is filled;
　　with the harvest of their lips they are satisfied.
21
The tongue has the power of life and death,
　　and those who love it will eat its fruit.
22
He who finds a wife finds what is good
　　and receives favor from the Lord.
23
The poor plead for mercy,
　　but the rich answer harshly.
24
One who has unreliable friends soon comes to ruin,
　　but there is a friend who sticks closer than a brother

CHAPTER 19

The Possible Outcome of "Love"

(Cheating, Hurt, Betrayal, Long suffering)

E motions are apart of life. They develop whether we want them to or not. We cannot help who we have a strong attraction to, but you can control how you react. When 2 people encounter each other and begin expressing feelings for one another, it is always butterflies and kissy faces in the beginning. One thing to remember is you both come from 2 totally different backgrounds and have different views of the world. Everybody has their own view of how they want to be treated by someone. You should know before you start interacting with boys the treatment you are willing to accept from them. You encounter obstacles in life so that you can learn from them to be prepared you for the next time it happens.

When you learn things, you can then be a blessing to help someone else go through the same situation. Remember: there is nothing new under the sun. Some people learn on the first encounter and implement what they learned into their life and some people take longer to realize the truth, so they keep doing the same thing expecting something different to happen. Ex: If your friends boyfriend continuously cheats and she believes he will change because she loves him too much to leave. The reason why he is not changing is because he is getting what he wants. Why should he stop? The question for her is: He does not value you, so why do you continue to stay? Regardless of what he is telling her baby girl, that's not love.

So, you must leave him the first time he does anything that disrespects you. For a boy to know, you are to be valuable, you must leave. It takes a moment to break trust but years to rebuild. If he loves you, he will do anything to get you back, if he doesn't attempt to, he wasn't for you. Brush it off and do not go back to that situation. Period. I know that sounds easier said than done but, once you realize your worth, it will become easier. Allow time to hurt for a little while but then fix your tiara and keep it moving. In time, all wounds will heal. Just remember to allow time for your heart to heal, by being alone. Do not think being in another relationship will heal you. Only God can heal your brokenness, but you are the overseer of your heart. No one can break it if you do not give it to them.

Prayer: Thank You, Lord, for allowing me to experience love and hurt and heal my heart as I continue to worship you. In Jesus' name, Amen.

Proverbs 19

1
Better the poor whose walk is blameless
   than a fool whose lips are perverse.
2
Desire without knowledge is not good—
   how much more will hasty feet miss the way!
3
A person's own folly leads to their ruin,
   yet their heart rages against the Lord.
4
Wealth attracts many friends,
   but even the closest friend of the poor person deserts them.
5
A false witness will not go unpunished,
   and whoever pours out lies will not go free.
6
Many curry favor with a ruler,
   and everyone is the friend of one who gives gifts.

7

The poor are shunned by all their relatives—
  how much more do their friends avoid them!
Though the poor pursue them with pleading,
  they are nowhere to be found.[a]

8

The one who gets wisdom loves life;
  the one who cherishes understanding will soon prosper.

9

A false witness will not go unpunished,
  and whoever pours out lies will perish.

10

It is not fitting for a fool to live in luxury—
  how much worse for a slave to rule over princes!

11

A person's wisdom yields patience;
  it is to one's glory to overlook an offense.

12

A king's rage is like the roar of a lion,
  but his favor is like dew on the grass.

13

A foolish child is a father's ruin,
  and a quarrelsome wife is like
  the constant dripping of a leaky roof.

14

Houses and wealth are inherited from parents,
  but a prudent wife is from the Lord.

15

Laziness brings on deep sleep,
  and the shiftless go hungry.

16

Whoever keeps commandments keeps their life,
  but whoever shows contempt for their ways will die.

17

Whoever is kind to the poor lends to the Lord,
  and he will reward them for what they have done.

18

Discipline your children, for in that there is hope;
    do not be a willing party to their death.

19

A hot-tempered person must pay the penalty;
    rescue them, and you will have to do it again.

20

Listen to advice and accept discipline,
    and at the end you will be counted among the wise.

21

Many are the plans in a person's heart,
    but it is the Lord's purpose that prevails.

22

What a person desires is unfailing love[b];
    better to be poor than a liar.

23

The fear of the Lord leads to life;
    then one rests content, untouched by trouble.

24

A sluggard buries his hand in the dish;
    he will not even bring it back to his mouth!

25

Flog a mocker, and the simple will learn prudence;
    rebuke the discerning, and they will gain knowledge.

26

Whoever robs their father and drives out their mother
    is a child who brings shame and disgrace.

27

Stop listening to instruction, my son,
    and you will stray from the words of knowledge.

28

A corrupt witness mocks at justice,
    and the mouth of the wicked gulps down evil.

29

Penalties are prepared for mockers,
    and beatings for the backs of fools.

CHAPTER 20

The Different Kinds of Friends

Friends come and go but for the real ones, keep them close while staying true and loyal to them. There is a difference between an associate and a friend. A friend is someone who you can count on, in your time of need and lean on by being a shoulder to cry on. Someone you can tell your vulnerable moments to without them being exposed to the world. Someone who you can call, and you know they are willing to do the dumb thing that you shouldn't even be doing but they will do it because they're your side kick. Example: When I was younger and I had a boyfriend (pure waste of time) and I had this one friend who no matter what time, she was down for whatever. If I had an itching to do a swing by (drive past my boyfriend's house to see if his car was home) she was always ready. "Give me 5 minutes then come get me" was her favorite line. No matter how much she told me to leave him alone. She was always there in the passenger seat. All the time my intuition was right. This is a reason why I said wait to date and trust yourself. It will save you some heartache, and a peace of mind. Those friends don't come by often so when you get them hold on to them.

When it comes to friends, learn to let go of the small things and make sure they respect the friendship just as much as you do. Meaning are they a one-sided friend, do they always need a favor but when you ask them for something they aren't available or don't want to do it. Do not let it be a one-sided friendship. A true friend is someone who may get on your nerves for the choices they make or things they say, but you love them the same. You can disagree and still call each other in a few days. You can lose contact and jump right back into the swing of things once reconnected. The love is real. You never know when you will bump into them and need them. True Friends are always your friends. They are always there when you need them, and they understand when you need time apart to better your situation. But True Friends will always find their way back to one another. Like magnets. A true friend is hard to come by. A true friend is your friend regardless of your flaws.

An associate is someone who you speak to during a certain class or just at specific times; someone you don't really keep in contact with but are cordial with when you are around them. Like a classmate, co-worker or a church buddy. Someone who is a situational friend is based on the current situation is the main reason you both communicate. Basically, an associate is someone you are friendly with.

Ok let us talk male friends. A male friend is possible but be wise. Some guys have ulterior motives and will be your friend until they feel like they want to take the chance. There will sometimes be a physical attraction between a male and a female so you must make sure that you stick to the friendship rules. There must be boundaries in this type of friendship. If this is your friend, then he is strictly your friend. There cannot be any sexual or romantic activity at all to be a real friend. Real friends do not do those things together. So, make sure when you categorize your male friends you do not use this "friend" label loosely. Any male you have sexual encounters with, you and he are no longer "just friends," because if you crossed that line once, it is a possibility you will cross it again and different feelings may begin to evolve. Let's say you are old enough to date, you start a relationship and it begins to get serious, if you have had sex with your "friend" (which you shouldn't even be thinking about) but you did, that's one of the first things your new boo is going to ask. Then you will have an issue with dating and possibly miss out on the guy God has planned for you because you will always have to choose. Best advice be truthful about your friendship, and if he is secure with that situation knowing all the details, then ok. Second, you must think about it like this would you be secure with your boyfriend hanging around someone who they have crossed that line with? So, don't put yourself in that situation. Avoid it at all costs. If that is your friend don't cross that line: Just be a friend and make it clear.

Prayer: Thank you, Lord, for the friends you have placed in my life. Remove who is not for me and place only people who you are for me. In Jesus' name, Amen.

Proverbs 20

1
Wine is a mocker and beer a brawler;
  whoever is led astray by them is not wise.
2
A king's wrath strikes terror like the roar of a lion;
  those who anger him forfeit their lives.
3
It is to one's honor to avoid strife,
  but every fool is quick to quarrel.
4
Sluggards do not plow in season;
  so at harvest time they look but find nothing.
5
The purposes of a person's heart are deep waters,
  but one who has insight draws them out.
6
Many claim to have unfailing love,
  but a faithful person who can find?
7
The righteous lead blameless lives;
  blessed are their children after them.
8
When a king sits on his throne to judge,
  he winnows out all evil with his eyes.

9
Who can say, "I have kept my heart pure;
    I am clean and without sin"?
10
Differing weights and differing measures—
    the Lord detests them both.
11
Even small children are known by their actions,
    so is their conduct really pure and upright?
12
Ears that hear and eyes that see—
    the Lord has made them both.
13
Do not love sleep or you will grow poor;
    stay awake and you will have food to spare.
14
"It's no good, it's no good!" says the buyer—
    then goes off and boasts about the purchase.
15
Gold there is, and rubies in abundance,
    but lips that speak knowledge are a rare jewel.
16
Take the garment of one who puts up security for a stranger;
    hold it in pledge if it is done for an outsider.
17
Food gained by fraud tastes sweet,
    but one ends up with a mouth full of gravel.
18
Plans are established by seeking advice;
    so if you wage war, obtain guidance.
19
A gossip betrays a confidence;
    so avoid anyone who talks too much.
20
If someone curses their father or mother,
    their lamp will be snuffed out in pitch darkness.

21

An inheritance claimed too soon
  will not be blessed at the end.

22

Do not say, "I'll pay you back for this wrong!"
  Wait for the Lord, and he will avenge you.

23

The Lord detests differing weights,
  and dishonest scales do not please him.

24

A person's steps are directed by the Lord.
  How then can anyone understand their own way?

25

It is a trap to dedicate something rashly
  and only later to consider one's vows.

26

A wise king winnows out the wicked;
  he drives the threshing wheel over them.

27

The human spirit is[a] the lamp of the Lord
  that sheds light on one's inmost being.

28

Love and faithfulness keep a king safe;
  through love his throne is made secure.

29

The glory of young men is their strength,
  gray hair the splendor of the old.

30

Blows and wounds scrub away evil,
  and beatings purge the inmost being.

High School Blues

CHAPTER 21

High School

Oh boy, oh boy, the high school years! These are often the most fun and most memorable years of every individual's life. These are the years of building your character as you become an adult. It is the beginning of knowing how you are willing and unwilling to accept treatment from others. I told my oldest daughter before she started middle school, "you must teach people how to treat you by not accepting your definition of mistreatment." The older generation have said for a long time, "treat people as you want to be treated." As we know in 2021 that's not so true anymore as the world is evolving, we can no longer go by that saying. You should now, treat people as they want to be treated, because after elementary school people have their own way they want to be treated and perceived. Something that will help you along your journey is to take these years to get to know people for who they are. Everyone is different, you all come from different backgrounds, family styles, and cultures. So, accept them for who they are and do not set expectations for anyone. A major key to life and interaction with others is establishing this characteristic now, it will help you with understanding people.

Being a doer of your word means walk the walk and not just talk the talk. Do not just say what sounds good, say it because you mean it. Hence, the saying, "say what you mean and mean what you say." Keeping your word is what builds your credibility when you have none. I learned this by being on the other side. It taught me early to believe someone when they show you who they really are. You do not really know someone until you don't give them what they want. The best way to see someone's true color is to tell them "No." You do not ever have to be a doormat to anyone. Meaning don't allow people to walk over you and dictate how you live life. Once you allow them to walk over you, they will not stop. You have allowed them to form this idea that I did it before I can do it again.

To sum this up, learn how to deal with different people because high school is a mixing bowl of different types of people. It's preparing you for the real world. You're not going to be able to pick who you work with until you own your own business. (Yes Boo, speak it into existence) Learn now, how to be cordial with with people you do not care for or the person who you feel you can't stand. Be kind to everyone because that's what the Lord wants and you never know what the next person is being treated at home. Leaving home and going to school might just be the only peace someone has. You shouldn't want to take that peace from them.

High school should teach you how to be a real friend or show you the qualities you lack as a friend. As you begin to go through different situations with your friends, you will see what you want and don't want to be involved in and what you chose and chose not to deal with. You are to stay loyal to your friends and understand that you are all unique, each having their own flaws and beliefs. Understanding that you will not always see eye to eye but, if you're loyal and true, you will make it work. Always be honest to your friends. Not just sometimes when you don't want to hurt their feelings, but all the time. It's better to hurt their feelings in private then someone else hurt them in public. Emotions are temporary so, just be honest. Be wise in honesty. Wise means to be mindful of how you deliver the honest information. Pray about things before you express them. Ask the Lord to give you the words to say that will not hurt or harm the person who needs to receive the information.

Prayer: Thank you, Father, for allowing me to make it to high school. Help me to learn the things I will need for the future that you have in store for me and give me strength to endure the years to come. In Jesus' name, Amen.

Proverbs 21

1
In the Lord's hand the king's heart is a stream of water
    that he channels toward all who please him.
2
A person may think their own ways are right,
    but the Lord weighs the heart.
3
To do what is right and just
    is more acceptable to the Lord than sacrifice.
4
Haughty eyes and a proud heart—
    the unplowed field of the wicked—produce sin.
5
The plans of the diligent lead to profit
    as surely as haste leads to poverty.
6
A fortune made by a lying tongue
    is a fleeting vapor and a deadly snare.[a]
7
The violence of the wicked will drag them away,
    for they refuse to do what is right.
8
The way of the guilty is devious,
    but the conduct of the innocent is upright.
9
Better to live on a corner of the roof
    than share a house with a quarrelsome wife.
10
The wicked crave evil;
    their neighbors get no mercy from them.
11
When a mocker is punished, the simple gain wisdom;
    by paying attention to the wise they get knowledge.

12
The Righteous One[b] takes note of the house of the wicked
   and brings the wicked to ruin.
13
Whoever shuts their ears to the cry of the poor
   will also cry out and not be answered.
14
A gift given in secret soothes anger,
   and a bribe concealed in the cloak pacifies great wrath.
15
When justice is done, it brings joy to the righteous
   but terror to evildoers.
16
Whoever strays from the path of prudence
   comes to rest in the company of the dead.
17
Whoever loves pleasure will become poor;
   whoever loves wine and olive oil will never be rich.
18
The wicked become a ransom for the righteous,
   and the unfaithful for the upright.
19
Better to live in a desert
   than with a quarrelsome and nagging wife.
20
The wise store up choice food and olive oil,
   but fools gulp theirs down.
21
Whoever pursues righteousness and love
   finds life, prosperity[c] and honor.
22
One who is wise can go up against the city of the mighty
   and pull down the stronghold in which they trust.
23
Those who guard their mouths and their tongues
   keep themselves from calamity.

24

The proud and arrogant person—"Mocker" is his name—
  behaves with insolent fury.

25

The craving of a sluggard will be the death of him,
  because his hands refuse to work.

26

All day long he craves for more,
  but the righteous give without sparing.

27

The sacrifice of the wicked is detestable—
  how much more so when brought with evil intent!

28

A false witness will perish,
  but a careful listener will testify successfully.

29

The wicked put up a bold front,
  but the upright give thought to their ways.

30

There is no wisdom, no insight, no plan
  that can succeed against the Lord.

31

The horse is made ready for the day of battle,
  but victory rests with the Lord.

CHAPTER 22

Mean Girls!

Repeat x3: I will love my sisters as Christ loves me.

We all have it in us to be a mean girl, but it is a choice. Just like it's a choice to choose to be happy or wake up and put on a purple shirt with some black ripped jeans and your purple Jordan's. Don't be a mean girl. A mean girl is the one who puts people down because of what they look like, what they wear, where they live, how they speak, how smart they aren't-all negative comes out when she opens her mouth.

People are going to talk about you regardless because that's what most high school girls do, so decide to be the girl that everyone talks about because you're always happy and delivering some uplifting motivation to someone right on time. I would hate for you to have to be the one to ever say "I could've been nicer to the girl who just committed suicide." You never know who may be contemplating this action and the next words expressed to her would be the deciding factor. Display kindness to everyone at all costs. It is very true, if you have nothing nice to say then don't say anything at all. She may not be strong enough to keep a positive outlook on life when she goes home to mental and sexual abuse then tries to find peace at school. Then, just as she feels she has escaped harms way, she is ridiculed by her peers. That is a lot for anyone to deal with. Show her Jesus through you to give her hope, because trouble doesn't last always. There is light at the end of her tunnel, baby girl, hold on.

Paraphrasing Matthew 18:36-40 The Lord first commands you love the Lord with all your heart and second love thy neighbor as thyself. "Let's take care of each other instead of looking down upon one another. Just imagine the outcome if you expressed a good morning, have a blessed day or a simple "Jesus loves you" to the person who you don't know or just looks sad. Teenagers get depressed at times too. Just know, things will get better and they will not always be the way they are today. Sometimes saying the simplest statement or compliment to someone will make the biggest difference in their life. Always be positive and know things will work themselves out because God doesn't put more on us than we can handle. Just seek him and ask him to guide you through your struggles. Call on Jesus whenever you feel down or like there is no one else you can turn to. Trust in the lord with all your heart and lean not to your own understanding. Proverbs 3:5.New International Version.

Prayer: Lord, thank you for my life, the good and the bad, help me to speak life into someone from you through me. Help me to be the light from you to anyone in need. In Jesus name, Amen.

Proverbs 22

1
A good name is more desirable than great riches;
    to be esteemed is better than silver or gold.
2
Rich and poor have this in common:
    The Lord is the Maker of them all.
3
The prudent see danger and take refuge,
    but the simple keep going and pay the penalty.
4
Humility is the fear of the Lord;
    its wages are riches and honor and life.

5
In the paths of the wicked are snares and pitfalls,
   but those who would preserve their life stay far from them.
6
Start children off on the way they should go,
   and even when they are old they will not turn from it.
7
The rich rule over the poor,
   and the borrower is slave to the lender.
8
Whoever sows injustice reaps calamity,
   and the rod they wield in fury will be broken.
9
The generous will themselves be blessed,
   for they share their food with the poor.
10
Drive out the mocker, and out goes strife;
   quarrels and insults are ended.
11
One who loves a pure heart and who speaks with grace
   will have the king for a friend.
12
The eyes of the Lord keep watch over knowledge,
   but he frustrates the words of the unfaithful.
13
The sluggard says, "There's a lion outside!
   I'll be killed in the public square!"
14
The mouth of an adulterous woman is a deep pit;
   a man who is under the Lord's wrath falls into it.
15
Folly is bound up in the heart of a child,
   but the rod of discipline will drive it far away.
16
One who oppresses the poor to increase his wealth
   and one who gives gifts to the rich—both come to poverty.

Thirty Sayings of the Wise
Saying 1
17
Pay attention and turn your ear to the sayings of the wise;
    apply your heart to what I teach,
18
for it is pleasing when you keep them in your heart
    and have all of them ready on your lips.
19
So that your trust may be in the Lord,
    I teach you today, even you.
20
Have I not written thirty sayings for you,
    sayings of counsel and knowledge,
21
teaching you to be honest and to speak the truth,
    so that you bring back truthful reports
    to those you serve?
Saying 2
22
Do not exploit the poor because they are poor
    and do not crush the needy in court,
23
for the Lord will take up their case
    and will exact life for life.
Saying 3
24
Do not make friends with a hot-tempered person,
    do not associate with one easily angered,
25
or you may learn their ways
    and get yourself ensnared.
Saying 4
26
Do not be one who shakes hands in pledge
    or puts up security for debts;

27

if you lack the means to pay,
    your very bed will be snatched from under you.

Saying 5

28

Do not move an ancient boundary stone
    set up by your ancestors.

Saying 6

29

Do you see someone skilled in their work?
    They will serve before kings;
    they will not serve before officials of low rank.

CHAPTER 23

Boys

Everybody must go through the processes of life to reach your destiny. We all have a divine purpose and until we find that purpose, we are trying to allow the Lord to direct us on the path. Boys must be boys to become the men they need to be for women. Let them be boys and, until they can prove that they are worth your time, DO NOT give it to them. I repeat… DO NOT waste your time on Boys. Boys will always be there, it's not like there is a shortage. I only say that because, Boys are a distraction. A distraction is something that throws you off the path laid out for you. Avoid distractions at all costs. You can be friends if you know that you are disciplined enough to be just that: A friend.

Boys will be your downfall throughout your life if you allow them. Some boys have a good male role model which hopefully shows them how to be a man and teaches them how to provide, protect and properly treat a woman. The statement a woman can not raise a man is true. Later in life, when choosing a life partner, pay attention to boys raised by a single mother. Shout Out to all my single mothers doing the best they can to raise these boys. From an outsider looking into the situation I believe, single mothers of sons, you can only try to teach them how you would want a man to treat a woman but, ultimately, it takes a proper respectful man to raise a gentleman. As human nature goes, we learn from what we are shown. As a single mother to be able to raise a gentleman there must be a positive man around them so they will have an example. It can be their father, uncle, family friend or mentor. Just someone who can show them the way.

Not all, but most boys go through a phase of feeling like they should sell drugs, why because it's fast money and the idea that girls want the dude with the most money. So, most of them are going to at least think about it. Only the risk takers will try it. Note: A drug dealer and a hustler are different. Someone could be both or just one. A drug dealer is a dealer of illegal drugs. Hustling is a mentality, a hustler is always thinking of how to benefit from any and all situations. (Great future business owner) A hustler is good with words, a smooth talker and can make a deal out of anything. A hustle is so good with words they can sell you something that's already yours. Beware of them as well, if you aren't quick with words they will get you. They can manipulate any situation for their own good, to the point where they will end up having you do something that you know isn't what you intended to do or even wanted to do. They don't take "No" for an answer. They are the ones, the guys send over to soften the group of girls up before they all make there move. Every group has at least one. So again be cautious.

As young girls, you fall for the bad boys because they are usually popular and good looking. All the girls want them. So go ahead and let the other girls have them! You stay away from them. They mean you no good while they are acting on their selfish wants. Wait until you are older and they have learned to direct their hustling mentality towards business ventures! You will learn that everybody learns at their own timing and at their own pace. This is a process that cannot be rushed. Leave them alone. Boys are a distraction from your goal. Let them figure out what type of men they want to be known as before you involve your feelings, baby girl. This piece of advice will save you from years of unnecessary hurt.

Prayer: Thank you, Lord, for protecting me by allowing me stay focus and not be distracted by the right now and keep me focused on the goal. In Jesus name, Amen.

Proverbs 23

Saying 7
1
When you sit to dine with a ruler,
note well what[a] is before you,
2
and put a knife to your throat
if you are given to gluttony.
3
Do not crave his delicacies,
for that food is deceptive.
Saying 8
4
Do not wear yourself out to get rich;
do not trust your own cleverness.
5
Cast but a glance at riches, and they are gone,
for they will surely sprout wings
and fly off to the sky like an eagle.
Saying 9
6
Do not eat the food of a begrudging host,
do not crave his delicacies;
7
for he is the kind of person
who is always thinking about the cost.[b]
"Eat and drink," he says to you,
but his heart is not with you.
8
You will vomit up the little you have eaten
and will have wasted your compliments.
Saying 10
9
Do not speak to fools,
for they will scorn your prudent words.

Saying 11
10
Do not move an ancient boundary stone
   or encroach on the fields of the fatherless,
11
for their Defender is strong;
   he will take up their case against you.
Saying 12
12
Apply your heart to instruction
   and your ears to words of knowledge.
Saying 13
13
Do not withhold discipline from a child;
   if you punish them with the rod, they will not die.
14
Punish them with the rod
   and save them from death.
Saying 14
15
My son, if your heart is wise,
   then my heart will be glad indeed;
16
my inmost being will rejoice
   when your lips speak what is right.
Saying 15
17
Do not let your heart envy sinners,
   but always be zealous for the fear of the Lord.
18
There is surely a future hope for you,
   and your hope will not be cut off.
Saying 16
19
Listen, my son, and be wise,
   and set your heart on the right path:

20

Do not join those who drink too much wine
   or gorge themselves on meat,

21

for drunkards and gluttons become poor,
   and drowsiness clothes them in rags.

Saying 17

22

Listen to your father, who gave you life,
   and do not despise your mother when she is old.

23

Buy the truth and do not sell it—
   wisdom, instruction and insight as well.

24

The father of a righteous child has great joy;
   a man who fathers a wise son rejoices in him.

25

May your father and mother rejoice;
   may she who gave you birth be joyful!

Saying 18

26

My son, give me your heart
   and let your eyes delight in my ways,

27

for an adulterous woman is a deep pit,
   and a wayward wife is a narrow well.

28

Like a bandit she lies in wait
   and multiplies the unfaithful among men.

Saying 19

29

Who has woe? Who has sorrow?
   Who has strife? Who has complaints?
   Who has needless bruises? Who has bloodshot eyes?

30
Those who linger over wine,
   who go to sample bowls of mixed wine.
31
Do not gaze at wine when it is red,
   when it sparkles in the cup,
   when it goes down smoothly!
32
In the end it bites like a snake
   and poisons like a viper.
33
Your eyes will see strange sights,
   and your mind will imagine confusing things.
34
You will be like one sleeping on the high seas,
   lying on top of the rigging.
35
"They hit me," you will say, "but I'm not hurt!
   They beat me, but I don't feel it!
When will I wake up
   so I can find another drink?"

CHAPTER 24

Dating

Repeat x3: I am worthy of love, honor, and respect. I am valuable.

The primary purpose of dating is to get to know someone for the purpose of marriage. In middle and high school, you are still a child, being taken care of by your parents, you are unaware of who you are or who will become in 10 years. You may not even like who the person you are so "madly in love with" turns out to be. You don't even know who you are yet. Dating is dangerous for the heart as an adult so just imagine in the hands of children in high school. So, if you choose to risk it, be prepared for what is to come: a period of uneasiness. It is okay to be alone or just friends with boys in order to avoid getting your feelings hurt and to avoid the temptation of engaging in sexual behaviors. Sex is so much harder to fight when you have feelings for the other person who you may choose to be around a lot. Do not put yourself in the situation to be tempted. Temptations evolve from below. No one told me so I'm going to tell you: boys do not know what they want and most of them don't begin to choose to be serious until they become mature men. There is no set time when a man decides to be a family man, I wish someone would have told me this - it would have spared so many years of getting my feelings hurt.

Most men aren't tired of playing games or aren't ready to settle down until about 30 years old and sometimes later than that. So, now relate that to dating in high school, it's a gamble- some boys are raised to do right by women, raised with morals, to have respect for women or had a father in their life to guide them on how to treat a female, with love, honor, and respect. God willing, the one you like was taught that a man is to be a provider, to protect you and not harm you. Note: Boys are not supposed to hit girls was the motto when I was in high school. Sadly, as the times are changing, that is changing as well. Some young girls still are taught boys can't hit them, so they test it, but these boys are starting to hit back. Now you know for a fact, that boys are physically stronger than girls, so don't hit a boy unless you are prepared to be hit back. Some boy's parents aren't teaching them to not hit girls anymore. It's all about defending yourself because some of these girls aren't so girlie anymore.

Moral of the message: please don't go into high school thinking every boy that says you're cute wants to do right by you, marry you, or has good intentions. Take your time, you will get to know someone better when y'all are just friends anyway. You will get to see the real person verses his representative, the person he may want you to see. If he isn't ok with that then he already has ulterior motives and doesn't respect your wishes. You deserve to be respected.

There will be many times, when you will feel you need a boyfriend to make you happy or for comfort especially when you don't have that love from your father. I hope by now you know that Jesus is the only man you need. Build up your self-love with affirmations to be able to love yourself enough to know you are so much better than anything these boys can offer you.

Pay attention to the music they listen to, those words become their truth. The things we put into our mind are an example of the actions we will or want to perform. Much of the music they play today is all about sex, being with this girl and that girl, getting money by robbing or selling drugs and nothing about respect or commitment to one person. They may try to say they don't even listen to the words they just like the beat, well just know the lyrics are subconsciously being downloaded into his brain whether he believes it or not. The worldly music has put it in every young boy's head that listens that it is the goal to have the most money and most girls. So, let them do that and don't be a casualty of that situation, boo. The popular or cute boys are the worst of them to be honest. They already know they can have any girl they want based on their looks so it's easier. In this world everybody focuses on the wrong things which is outer beauty and not the inner beauty. Someone could be so fine but have a stank personality. That's why God seeks your heart. He made us all perfect and just as he wanted us. Search for the love of the Lord not the love of man. He will never leave you.

If you choose to date despite my warnings, make sure you truly date him first before you commit to a relationship. Remember for anything to evolve, you must know yourself and then you must take time to get to know the other person. Everyone has flaws, the question is are you able to deal with his issues and is he willing to deal with yours? If you say ok and continue the relationship, then you need to figure out how communication works for you both as a couple. Look at it as you are teammates with the goal being success. You must be aware that you are both trying to figure these things out and if you haven't been shown an example of a healthy relationship then it's going to be harder to figure out. There are some questions to help you see if he is worth your time.

1. Does he love the Lord? (A MUST!)
2. Does he have 2 parents in his household? (This shows that he has had an example of how to treat women)
3. Are his parents still married? (To see if he had a family structure example)
4. How is his relationship with his mother and father? (Hopefully, his father is a positive role model and he respects his mom)
5. Does he show you respect? (Another must)
6. Do you feel valued? (Never stay anywhere you aren't valued)
7. Does he respect your body or try to touch you any chance he gets? (Actions speak louder than words)
8. Does he keep his word? (Your word is all you have)

Prayer: Thank you lord, for loving me despite of my flaws. I trust you Lord, I love you Lord, in Jesus name Amen.

Proverb 24

Saying 20

1

Do not envy the wicked,
    do not desire their company;

2

for their hearts plot violence,
    and their lips talk about making trouble.

Saying 21

3

By wisdom a house is built,
    and through understanding it is established;

4

through knowledge its rooms are filled
    with rare and beautiful treasures.

Saying 22

5

The wise prevail through great power,
    and those who have knowledge muster their strength.

6

Surely you need guidance to wage war,
    and victory is won through many advisers.

Saying 23

7

Wisdom is too high for fools;
    in the assembly at the gate they must not open their mouths.

Saying 24

8

Whoever plots evil
    will be known as a schemer.

9

The schemes of folly are sin,
    and people detest a mocker.

Saying 25

10

If you falter in a time of trouble,
  how small is your strength!

11

Rescue those being led away to death;
  hold back those staggering toward slaughter.

12

If you say, "But we knew nothing about this,"
  does not he who weighs the heart perceive it?
Does not he who guards your life know it?
  Will he not repay everyone according to what they have done?

Saying 26

13

Eat honey, my son, for it is good;
  honey from the comb is sweet to your taste.

14

Know also that wisdom is like honey for you:
  If you find it, there is a future hope for you,
  and your hope will not be cut off.

Saying 27

15

Do not lurk like a thief near the house of the righteous,
  do not plunder their dwelling place;

16

for though the righteous fall seven times, they rise again,
  but the wicked stumble when calamity strikes.

Saying 28

17

Do not gloat when your enemy falls;
  when they stumble, do not let your heart rejoice,

18

or the Lord will see and disapprove
  and turn his wrath away from them.

Saying 29

19

Do not fret because of evildoers
  or be envious of the wicked,

20

for the evildoer has no future hope,
  and the lamp of the wicked will be snuffed out.

Saying 30

21

Fear the Lord and the king, my son,
  and do not join with rebellious officials,

22

for those two will send sudden destruction on them,
  and who knows what calamities they can bring?

Further Sayings of the Wise

23 These also are sayings of the wise:

To show partiality in judging is not good:

24

Whoever says to the guilty, "You are innocent,"
  will be cursed by peoples and denounced by nations.

25

But it will go well with those who convict the guilty,
  and rich blessing will come on them.

26

An honest answer
  is like a kiss on the lips.

27

Put your outdoor work in order
  and get your fields ready;
  after that, build your house.

28

Do not testify against your neighbor without cause—
  would you use your lips to mislead?

29

Do not say, "I'll do to them as they have done to me;
  I'll pay them back for what they did."

30

I went past the field of a sluggard,
   past the vineyard of someone who has no sense;

31

thorns had come up everywhere,
   the ground was covered with weeds,
   and the stone wall was in ruins.

32

I applied my heart to what I observed
   and learned a lesson from what I saw:

33

A little sleep, a little slumber,
   a little folding of the hands to rest—

34

and poverty will come on you like a thief
   and scarcity like an armed man.

CHAPTER 25

Fornication (sex before marriage)

Before I begin this chapter, let's not forget the target age range for this book is 12-18 years old. So, unless you're married this chapter applies to you. As we know the world glorifies unprotected sex by making shows glorifying teen pregnancy, songs glorifying fornication, pornography and so much more. It's hard as parents to keep a child focused on education daily without all the extra outside influence. Teens are being confused if they do not know what the words of the bible say.

Sex should be between a husband and a wife. If you are not married then you need to refrain from this act, because so much more comes with sex than pleasure. 1. False feelings (sex has a way of making you believe the feelings are stronger than they really are). Creating a false sense of entrapment in a situation ship – defined as this is just something we do, no commitment. 2. Babies (unplanned pregnancies),. 3. Diseases (sexually transmitted diseases can be a lifelong regret or a temporary discomfort), 4. HIV / AIDS (the wages of sin are death, when it is a possibility to prevent, prevent it at all costs). To be fair, we all may have slipped and fallen short when curiosity peaks and wanting to fit in. We also didn't make the best decisions either. Therefore, you have been given your parents to guide you and advise you before you make the same bad decisions.

So, I'm not going to be a hypocrite, I was lost as a teenager, unaware and uninformed that all I needed was the Lord. I grew up without my father in my life, believing I knew it all which turned into me becoming a rebellious teenage girl who never even thought anything like that would happen to me, but it did. When I was 15 years old, I became curious and started to have unprotected sex with my boyfriend. I took a pregnancy test in school and found out I was pregnant. I was too scared to tell my mom, so I hid it as long as I could. Until one day my frenemy (friend/enemy) called my house, (we didn't have cell phones yet) and told her I was pregnant. Can you say mad?! I had to tell her it was a lie, and she believed me. The guilt drove me crazy, so I wrote my mom a long letter confessing my pregnancy. She sat us both down and told me how disappointed she was and that hurt me because I'm the middle and favorite child, sorry Tenesha and Bridgetta. As time passed, I had my daughter, and it was hard trying to raise a child in high school but, thankfully, my mom helped me a lot. I'm so grateful for my mother and my sisters. Being a teen mom made me grow up faster than my peers because I had someone to be responsible for. I could no longer do the things I thought I wanted to do because of my daughter. I'm sharing this to let you know what can happen and what will happen if you go down the same path.

Remember: an adult decision comes with adult consequences. Sex is a reward of marriage. Save something special for your obedient walk. Not only because of the negative consequences that may occur but because it's the right thing to do in the eyes of the Lord. The Lord has saved special things for special times, between a husband and his wife like to be fruitful and multiply. Sex is not meant for pleasure-it's for a purpose. Remember the rhyme: "Johnny and Katie sitting in the tree K-I-S-S-I-N-G, first comes love, then comes marriage, then comes the baby in the baby carriage." It's supposed to happen in that order. You will be blessed if you stick to the Lord's plan for your life which is far greater than your own plans you have for yourself.

Prayer: Thank you, Lord for loving me, despite the bad choices I may make. Help me to flee from temptation and stay on the path you have laid for me. In Jesus' name, Amen

Proverbs 25

More Proverbs of Solomon
1
These are more proverbs of Solomon, compiled by the men of Hezekiah
king of Judah:
2
It is the glory of God to conceal a matter;
    to search out a matter is the glory of kings.
3
As the heavens are high and the earth is deep,
    so the hearts of kings are unsearchable.
4
Remove the dross from the silver,
    and a silversmith can produce a vessel;
5
remove wicked officials from the king's presence,
    and his throne will be established through righteousness.
6
Do not exalt yourself in the king's presence,
    and do not claim a place among his great men;
7
it is better for him to say to you, "Come up here,"
    than for him to humiliate you before his nobles.
What you have seen with your eyes
8
    do not bring[a]hastily to court
for what will you do in the end
    if your neighbor puts you to shame?
9
If you take your neighbor to court,
    do not betray another's confidence,
10
or the one who hears it may shame you
    and the charge against you will stand.

11
Like apples[b] of gold in settings of silver
  is a ruling rightly given.
12
Like an earring of gold or an ornament of fine gold
  is the rebuke of a wise judge to a listening ear.
13
Like a snow-cooled drink at harvest time
  is a trustworthy messenger to the one who sends him;
  he refreshes the spirit of his master.
14
Like clouds and wind without rain
  is one who boasts of gifts never given.
15
Through patience a ruler can be persuaded,
  and a gentle tongue can break a bone.
16
If you find honey, eat just enough—
  too much of it, and you will vomit.
17
Seldom set foot in your neighbor's house—
  too much of you, and they will hate you.
18
Like a club or a sword or a sharp arrow
  is one who gives false testimony against a neighbor.
19
Like a broken tooth or a lame foot
  is reliance on the unfaithful in a time of trouble.
20
Like one who takes away a garment on a cold day,
  or like vinegar poured on a wound,
  is one who sings songs to a heavy heart.
21
If your enemy is hungry, give him food to eat;
  if he is thirsty, give him water to drink.

22

In doing this, you will heap burning coals on his head,
  and the Lord will reward you.

23

Like a north wind that brings unexpected rain
  is a sly tongue—which provokes a horrified look.

24

Better to live on a corner of the roof
  than share a house with a quarrelsome wife.

25

Like cold water to a weary soul
  is good news from a distant land.

26

Like a muddied spring or a polluted well
  are the righteous who give way to the wicked.

27

It is not good to eat too much honey,
  nor is it honorable to search out matters that are too deep.

28

Like a city whose walls are broken through
  is a person who lacks self-control.

CHAPTER 26

Suicidal Thoughts / Never Give Up

Repeat X 3: Lord, give me strength because I am weak.

All good things come from the Lord and he is also able to make good from evil. Suicidal thoughts are thoughts to end what the Lord has created. These thoughts are from the devil, wanting you to believe that you do not matter. The devil is a liar. That is the farthest from the truth. The devil's sole purpose is to steal, kill, and destroy you from becoming all that the Lord has promised over your life. He is powerful but nowhere as near as powerful as your father in Heaven. The devil can make you believe that you are things that you are not and stop you from believing you can become all that the Lord has in store for you. Remember you matter to God. He created you for a divine purpose, you are a part of a bigger plan than you could ever imagine. You may not have discovered your purpose or can see the plans he has for you but that doesn't mean they don't exist; it is within you waiting to come out. Have faith, faith is the substance of things hoped for and the evidence of things not seen Hebrews 11:1 King James Version. God will not give you what you cannot handle, and he will not put anything on you that he has not planned to help you through.

So, remember, baby girl, there will be moments when you feel like life is too hard, you feel defeated, and you want to give up. That's when your breakthrough is about to come, don't give up, pray through the hurt. When you are at your lowest point the only way out is up. Look up to God and know that you are a child of the highest God and He is always with you. Speak to the Lord. He hears your cries, ask Him for what you are lacking, whatever it may be: peace, joy, hope, strength, love, courage, healing, when you believe He will provide. Sometimes Instantly. Build a relationship with God by reading his promises and His word. He is and always will be the only one you need. When you seek him, he will find you. I know He loves you; you need to believe He loves you too. All he wants is for you to believe in Him, come to Him surrendering your all. Don't ever feel like you have no value, or you don't deserve to live! Love yourself before you love anyone else BUT God!! Never allow anyone to take your joy. Never give anyone that much power over your life. You are in control of your feelings; you feel how you want to feel and own it. Give any problems and pain to the highest God and he will make everything ok. Try it and see.

Prayer: Thank you, Lord, for never leaving me. Help me to be strong and seek you whenever I feel alone. Provide me with the strength to endure long suffering. In Jesus' name, Amen.

Proverbs 26

1
Like snow in summer or rain in harvest,
   honor is not fitting for a fool.
2
Like a fluttering sparrow or a darting swallow,
   an undeserved curse does not come to rest.
3
A whip for the horse, a bridle for the donkey,
   and a rod for the backs of fools!

4

Do not answer a fool according to his folly,
   or you yourself will be just like him.

5

Answer a fool according to his folly,
   or he will be wise in his own eyes.

6

Sending a message by the hands of a fool
   is like cutting off one's feet or drinking poison.

7

Like the useless legs of one who is lame
   is a proverb in the mouth of a fool.

8

Like tying a stone in a sling
   is the giving of honor to a fool.

9

Like a thornbush in a drunkard's hand
   is a proverb in the mouth of a fool.

10

Like an archer who wounds at random
   is one who hires a fool or any passer-by.

11

As a dog returns to its vomit,
   so fools repeat their folly.

12

Do you see a person wise in their own eyes?
   There is more hope for a fool than for them.

13

A sluggard says, "There's a lion in the road,
   a fierce lion roaming the streets

14

As a door turns on its hinges,
   so a sluggard turns on his bed.

15

A sluggard buries his hand in the dish;
   he is too lazy to bring it back to his mouth.

16
A sluggard is wiser in his own eyes
than seven people who answer discreetly.
17
Like one who grabs a stray dog by the ears
is someone who rushes into a quarrel not their own.
18
Like a maniac shooting
flaming arrows of death
19
is one who deceives their neighbor
and says, "I was only joking!"
20
Without wood a fire goes out;
without a gossip a quarrel dies down.
21
As charcoal to embers and as wood to fire,
so is a quarrelsome person for kindling strife.
22
The words of a gossip are like choice morsels;
they go down to the inmost parts.
23
Like a coating of silver dross on earthenware
are fervent[a] lips with an evil heart.
24
Enemies disguise themselves with their lips,
but in their hearts they harbor deceit.
25
Though their speech is charming, do not believe them,
for seven abominations fill their hearts.
26
Their malice may be concealed by deception,
but their wickedness will be exposed in the assembly.

27

Whoever digs a pit will fall into it;

    if someone rolls a stone, it will roll back on them.

28

A lying tongue hates those it hurts,

    and a flattering mouth works ruin

CHAPTER 27

High School love may not evolve into real love

L ove is an emotion that matures over time, it takes: 1. Knowing how much love our Father, Our Lord and savior Jesus Christ has for each of us and 2. Maturity by encountering real life experiences to be able to endure the trials any relationship goes through and to obtain the tools needed to overcome them. Honestly, I thought I loved every boy I dated until I realized I really didn't know how to love someone. I had mistaken the initial feelings of the butterflies and thinking of the boy all the time in the beginning with love. Don't get it twisted, the initial feeling of real love seems like butterflies and roses but maintaining real love is hard and a forever changing process.

You must grow into love with someone. As you both grow and mature as individual people your level of understanding as a unit must grow as well. If you aren't ready to stick with somebody through the good, the bad and the hurtful times you aren't ready for love. I mean really, like the times when you feel like I can't take this anymore, to the point you want to leave, then you aren't ready to love just yet. Most high school love is temporary; there aren't many high school sweethearts that stay married for decades.

According to Brandon Gaille's study only 54 % of high school marriages last 10 years when married as a teenager, and 78% of high school sweethearts who married at 25 years old have a 10-year success rate. Why is this you ask? It's because when I was a child, I talked like a child, I thought like a child, I reasoned like a child. When I became a man, I put childish ways behind me. (1Corinthians 3:11 New International Version.

Again, it takes time for boys to mature into men. You cannot speed up this process and giving them ultimatums never work. As much as we would like them to, they have to mature on their own terms. Real love is patient, love is kind. It does not boast; it is not proud. It does not dishonor others, it is not self-seeking, it is not easily angered, it keeps no record of wrongs. Love does not delight in evil but rejoices with the truth. It always protects, always trust, always hopes, always persevere 1 Corinthians 3: 4-7 New International Version.

There are grown men still trying to figure this love thing out. Don't be surprised when the time comes you may have to kiss a lot of frogs to find your prince. However, love is a feeling that comes naturally and sometimes out of left field. Don't confuse time spent as love. If you spend enough time with anyone, you will eventually begin to have feelings for them, but love will come when the time is right. Don't rush it and don't waste your time. Your time is valuable and something you cannot get back so spend your time developing yourself. You are your biggest asset.

Prayer: Father, I thank you for allowing me to feel love, help me to seek your love above all, so I will be able to display your love in return.

Proverbs 27

1
Do not boast about tomorrow,
  for you do not know what a day may bring.
2
Let someone else praise you, and not your own mouth;
  an outsider, and not your own lips.

3

Stone is heavy and sand a burden,
    but a fool's provocation is heavier than both.

4

Anger is cruel and fury overwhelming,
    but who can stand before jealousy?

5

Better is open rebuke
    than hidden love.

6

Wounds from a friend can be trusted,
    but an enemy multiplies kisses.

7

One who is full loathes honey from the comb,
    but to the hungry even what is bitter tastes sweet.

8

Like a bird that flees its nest
    is anyone who flees from home.

9

Perfume and incense bring joy to the heart,
    and the pleasantness of a friend
    springs from their heartfelt advice.

10

Do not forsake your friend or a friend of your family,
    and do not go to your relative's house when disaster strikes you—
    better a neighbor nearby than a relative far away.

11

Be wise, my son, and bring joy to my heart;
    then I can answer anyone who treats me with contempt.

12

The prudent see danger and take refuge,
    but the simple keep going and pay the penalty.

13

Take the garment of one who puts up security for a stranger;
    hold it in pledge if it is done for an outsider.

14

If anyone loudly blesses their neighbor early in the morning,
    it will be taken as a curse.

15

A quarrelsome wife is like the dripping
    of a leaky roof in a rainstorm;

16

restraining her is like restraining the wind
    or grasping oil with the hand.

17

As iron sharpens iron,
    so one person sharpens another.

18

The one who guards a fig tree will eat its fruit,
    and whoever protects their master will be honored.

19

As water reflects the face,
    so one's life reflects the heart.[a]

20

Death and Destruction[b] are never satisfied,
    and neither are human eyes.

21

The crucible for silver and the furnace for gold,
    but people are tested by their praise.

22

Though you grind a fool in a mortar,
    grinding them like grain with a pestle,
    you will not remove their folly from them.

23

Be sure you know the condition of your flocks,
    give careful attention to your herds;

24

for riches do not endure forever,
    and a crown is not secure for all generations.

25

When the hay is removed and new growth appears
    and the grass from the hills is gathered in,

26

the lambs will provide you with clothing,
    and the goats with the price of a field.

27

You will have plenty of goats' milk to feed your family
    and to nourish your female servants.

Random Knowledge

CHAPTER 28

Money Management

Repeat X 3: I will learn to manage my money.

Money management is something that everyone struggles with still to this day, so to learn this early and start implementing it into your lifestyle will be so beneficial to you. I wasn't taught until I was 33yrs old how to budget my money and when I did it and I couldn't believe how much I had remaining, and I was no longer anticipating my paycheck. This is how I was taught to budget shown below. If money isn't accounted for before it's received it will be misused. Money goes quickly. As fast as you get it, it disappears. The root of all evil is the <u>lack of</u> and <u>the love</u> of money not just money in general. Don't let money control your behavior. Money changes people. It can make good people better or bad people worse. You choose who you will become.

Ok, Now let's talk Credit!!

Building credit: DO NOT- I repeat DO NOT get any credit cards unless they are secured. Unsecured credit cards will dig you into a hole that it takes a while to get out of. I say that because if you have $1,000 on a credit card you're going to spend it and then not want to pay it back, digging your hole of debt. A secured card can be used to build your credit. If you use a credit card, pay the full balance off every month, and don't spend more than half of the credit limit. Credit lenders want to see how much available credit you have. So, you can use the credit card to pay things like your phone bill, car note or gas. A bill that you know you have to pay anyway.

Loans: If you decide to take out a personal loan, car loan or mortgage. You can pay your loan off quicker by making your obligated payment that's your monthly payment and in 2 weeks make another payment of whatever amount you can afford to make, after making the payment call the lender and have them apply the full amount of the extra payment directly to your principal. If you don't call, they may apply the extra payment to the principal and interest and the interest would have eaten most of the payment. In doing this method, you will pay your loan off faster. Another way to build your credit quickly is to ask your parents (only if they have excellent credit) to add you as an authorized user on their credit card after a couple months your credit score should match their score. Good way to start your credit off to a good start. Then it's up to you to keep it good. Don't mess it up.

Let's talk about giving and saving!!!!

Tithing and Saving: You should be able to live off 70% of your take home income. An example of living off of 70% breaks down as follows, 10% give back to the Lord, 10% saved, 10 % pay yourself. The pay yourself account is the account once you build it up you can buy you something nice without digging into your savings. You should never touch your savings unless you are in urgent need. Follow this and watch how the Lord blesses you once you start to give with a giving heart. You may be hesitant because you feel as though you already don't have enough after paying your bills. Give back to the Lord first and watch how everything else falls into place. I bet you will never be without. Let me point out!! God doesn't need our money; he wants to see if you trust him to provide for you. All he is asking is for the first fruit. Meaning before you buy anything, pay a bill, anything. Once your money hits your hand you find a way to give your 10% to God. Giving is a generous act that the Lord expects of us. My Best Friend doesn't have a church home because he works 7 days a week, but his tithing is through people. He helps everyone all the time. He has a huge heart. So, give because you have and there are people who do not. Help whenever possible. Once I started tithing my 10 %, first, the Lord always provided. I never was in need. If I would have been taught how to manage money, pay tithes, build credit, obtain life insurance, and save money earlier in life I would absolutely be in a better place financial. Now that I understand how to do these things, I can teach the youth to help start them off right. We tithe in thankfulness to our Lord because it is God that provides our every need and through him, we can make money. New International Version Deuteronomy 26:10 says, "and now, O Lord, I have brought you the first portion of the harvest you have given me from the ground. Then place the produce before the Lord your God and bow to the ground in worship before him. We give with a thankful heart."

Let's talk Tax Refund!!!

Tax Refund!! If you worked and made more than $6,100 for the year (check IRS.gov, the amount may have changed) you must file income taxes. Income taxes are taxes that you pay during the year given back to you in a lump sum. Divided by Federal and state taxes. This lump sum of money returned to you, you should put some aside in your savings, invest in something or start businesses. If you spend it as fast as you get it, you're wasting it. This is usually the time of the year people buy what they been waiting to buy all year and spend so much money doing nothing but wasting money! If you have been properly saving and paying yourself, imagine how much money you will have by the time tax time comes. Tax time should be used to be for investing, buying land, buying property, stock, putting your money towards something that will get you money back in return. Think of how rich people stay rich. Don't buy anything that's not going to make you more money. Rich people spend their money wisely and most of them give to charities.

Let's talk budgeting!!!

Never go grocery shopping hungry, 10 times out of 10 you will end up spending extra money. Picking up stuff like confetti pancakes or mint flavored Oreos, things that sounded good at that time but eventually they go to waste in the Pantry. To resolve this problem, only take $5 over the amount you want to spend. Always make a list before you go shopping. Knowing the price of items so you know the total ahead of time. Use coupons and sign up for discounts. Know why you are at the store and stick to the plan.

Budgeting: When you start a job, you should implement this lay out. And as your bills pile up you can add them accordingly. Here is an example of a budgeting plan. Remember Pay the Lord First!!!

Example of How to set up Bills (Align the due dates with payday to make sure your bill is being paid before it is due.)

Monthly Bills	Due	Amount
Tithes (10%)	Every Check	$50
Phone	15th	$75
Car Note	20th	$150
Car Insurance	12th	$100
Gas	every 2 weeks	$50
Food	every 2 weeks	$150
Save	Monthly	$50
Pay yourself	Monthly	$50
	Monthly Bills	$665
	Total Income	$1000

Paycheck 1	30-Apr		Paycheck 2	May 15th
($500)			($500)	
Tithes (10 %)	$50		Tithes (10%)	$50
Gas	$50		Gas	$50
Insurance	$90		Car	$150
Save	$50		Pay Yourself	$50
Food	$75		Food	$75
Total Bills	$315		Total Bills	$375
Free Money	$185		Free Money	$125

If you follow this system, no payment will be late, and you will have extra money to spend while still being able to save some and put some away for a special day. The lord loves a cheerful giver. So, give with love.

Prayer: Thank you father for providing me the funds to be able to tithe to your kingdom, pay my bills and have money to spend. In Jesus name, Amen.

Proverbs 28

1
The wicked flee though no one pursues,
　　but the righteous are as bold as a lion.
2
When a country is rebellious, it has many rulers,
　　but a ruler with discernment and knowledge maintains order.
3
A ruler[a] who oppresses the poor
　　is like a driving rain that leaves no crops.
4
Those who forsake instruction praise the wicked,
　　but those who heed it resist them.
5
Evildoers do not understand what is right,
　　but those who seek the Lord understand it fully.
6
Better the poor whose walk is blameless
　　than the rich whose ways are perverse.
7
A discerning son heeds instruction,
　　but a companion of gluttons disgraces his father.
8
Whoever increases wealth by taking interest or profit from the poor
　　amasses it for another, who will be kind to the poor.

9
If anyone turns a deaf ear to my instruction,
    even their prayers are detestable.
10
Whoever leads the upright along an evil path
    will fall into their own trap,
        but the blameless will receive a good inheritance.
11
The rich are wise in their own eyes;
    one who is poor and discerning sees how deluded they are.
12
When the righteous triumph, there is great elation;
    but when the wicked rise to power, people go into hiding.
13
Whoever conceals their sins does not prosper,
    but the one who confesses and renounces them finds mercy.
14
Blessed is the one who always trembles before God,
    but whoever hardens their heart falls into trouble.
15
Like a roaring lion or a charging bear
    is a wicked ruler over a helpless people.
16
A tyrannical ruler practices extortion,
    but one who hates ill-gotten gain will enjoy a long reign.
17
Anyone tormented by the guilt of murder
    will seek refuge in the grave;
        let no one hold them back.
18
The one whose walk is blameless is kept safe,
    but the one whose ways are perverse will fall into the pit.[b]
19
Those who work their land will have abundant food,
    but those who chase fantasies will have their fill of poverty.

20

A faithful person will be richly blessed,
 but one eager to get rich will not go unpunished.

21

To show partiality is not good—
 yet a person will do wrong for a piece of bread.

22

The stingy are eager to get rich
 and are unaware that poverty awaits them.

23

Whoever rebukes a person will in the end gain favor
 rather than one who has a flattering tongue.

24

Whoever robs their father or mother
 and says, "It's not wrong,"
 is partner to one who destroys.

25

The greedy stir up conflict,
 but those who trust in the Lord will prosper.

26

Those who trust in themselves are fools,
 but those who walk in wisdom are kept safe.

27

Those who give to the poor will lack nothing,
 but those who close their eyes to them receive many curses.

28

When the wicked rise to power, people go into hiding;
 but when the wicked perish, the righteous thrive.

CHAPTER 29

Your Starter Jobs have a Purpose

Repeat x 3: Thank you lord for my job.

All teenagers want to work because you want your own money and to feel a sense of independence. My daughter's main goal for getting a job was to get her own phone and be able to pay the bill. She had the idea that I can't take it away when she got get in trouble. So I got her a phone plan, which took a bill off of my plate. What you can do is start taking the weight off your parents and buy your own clothes, hygiene products and or things you need to comfortable. Not just the games systems or toys you want. A job develops some responsibility within you. Now you must be responsible for getting to work on time, following rules outside of your parents' home and school. At the same time learning how to deal with different people and realize how fast money goes.

Everything we go through in life is to learn and teach us for our greater purpose down the road, especially your jobs. All the nuggets we pick up along the way are used for our good at the end of our journey. This is the beginning of the lessons of the value of a dollar and that as fast as money is earned, it is spent.

You should pick a job in which you enjoy doing. If you don't care for people, customer service is not for you. If you don't like animals, working in a vet clinic is not for you. Find a job where you can learn and perfect that skill, while acquiring the skills needed to perform that job, you are also preparing your future, all your saved tax refunds and saved money that you have accumulated over the years, you can put forth to start your own business. This is what saving your money, is for, so you can spend it on something to make you more money. To be fruitful in a business it takes consistency, persistence, and stability. You will need to able to endure the ups and the downs and do what it takes to succeed in your business. Take these years to find out what you like to do or are good at doing and make it into a business.

Prayer: Thank you, Lord, for blessing me with the opportunity to work and take some of the burden off my parents back. Guide me into being the best steward of my finances. In Jesus' name, Amen.

Proverbs 29

1
Whoever remains stiff-necked after many rebukes
  will suddenly be destroyed—without remedy.
2
When the righteous thrive, the people rejoice;
  when the wicked rule, the people groan.
3
A man who loves wisdom brings joy to his father,
  but a companion of prostitutes squanders his wealth.
4
By justice a king gives a country stability,
  but those who are greedy for[a] bribes tear it down.
5
Those who flatter their neighbors
  are spreading nets for their feet.

6
Evildoers are snared by their own sin,
   but the righteous shout for joy and are glad.
7
The righteous care about justice for the poor,
   but the wicked have no such concern.
8
Mockers stir up a city,
   but the wise turn away anger.
9
If a wise person goes to court with a fool,
   the fool rages and scoffs, and there is no peace.
10
The bloodthirsty hate a person of integrity
   and seek to kill the upright.
11
Fools give full vent to their rage,
   but the wise bring calm in the end.
12
If a ruler listens to lies,
   all his officials become wicked.
13
The poor and the oppressor have this in common:
   The Lord gives sight to the eyes of both.
14
If a king judges the poor with fairness,
   his throne will be established forever.
15
A rod and a reprimand impart wisdom,
   but a child left undisciplined disgraces its mother.
16
When the wicked thrive, so does sin,
   but the righteous will see their downfall.
17
Discipline your children, and they will give you peace;
   they will bring you the delights you desire.

18

Where there is no revelation, people cast off restraint;
    but blessed is the one who heeds wisdom's instruction.

19

Servants cannot be corrected by mere words;
    though they understand, they will not respond.

20

Do you see someone who speaks in haste?
    There is more hope for a fool than for them.

21

A servant pampered from youth
    will turn out to be insolent.

22

An angry person stirs up conflict,
    and a hot-tempered person commits many sins.

23

Pride brings a person low,
    but the lowly in spirit gain honor.

24

The accomplices of thieves are their own enemies;
    they are put under oath and dare not testify.

25

Fear of man will prove to be a snare,
    but whoever trusts in the Lord is kept safe.

26

Many seek an audience with a ruler,
    but it is from the Lord that one gets justice.

27

The righteous detest the dishonest;
    the wicked detest the upright.

CHAPTER 30

Listen to that inner voice, it's God!

Repeat X 3: I will listen and trust you Lord…

Your life is going in the direction the Lord is directing it go because once you make the decision to surrender to God you are giving Him total control. Life is a continual learning process with your final destination being Heaven. Although you get to decide how your life will be. You can go the way of truth and life or you can go the way of sin and destruction. Based on what you decide, everything is being tallied up in your personalized life book. A book of questions like: Were you kind to others? Did you give to the less fortunate, Did you pray without ceasing, Did you listen when God spoke to you? It may have taken 10 times but did you pass that test that God sent you?

Always follow your heart and be selfless (unselfish). Live by this scripture, nothing will be impossible with God. (Luke 1:37) Always trust that gut feeling within you that says go this way, take your umbrella and its a sunny day, don't do that, don't stop at this gas station stop at the next one, pick up that extra pair of gloves or whatever it is. That small still voice within, it's the Lord trying to prepare or protect you for what is to come. You may think it's silly at first until you keep ignoring it and then you see you should have listened all along. Start listening to Him.

One way God speaks to us is in our thoughts. That simple thought will prevent you from saying, "something told me". Trust God and do what the lord is telling you. He is that "something." It will not make sense at the time but eventually it will. When you don't trust the Lord and you start to ignore his signs because his path isn't what you want to do, or you doubt why you need to do it, His voice will become quieter and quieter and He eventually stop speaking to you, until you seek him whole heartedly again. He will never leave you, but you have to diligently seek the Lord above all things. God is our father, so believe, just as your parents warn you, your father in heaven warns you, time and time again. Once He realizes, just as our parents realize, you're going to do what you choose to do regardless of the warning signs, He steps back and lets you direct your own path knowing He will be there to pick up the pieces. Since you think this is your plan, let's see how well it works out. Again, all it takes is one bad decision to ruin your life. Don't be the one who has to say, "I knew I should've listened." Start today and listen.

Prayer: Thank you, Lord, for protecting me and helping me to make good decisions as I walk through my journey. I love you, Lord, and I give you all access over my life. Help me to be more like you. In Jesus' name, Amen.

Proverbs 30

Sayings of Agur
    221Thesayingsof Agursonof   Jakeh—aninspiredutterance
This man's utterance to Ithiel:
"I am weary, God,
    but I can prevail.[a]
2
Surely I am only a brute, not a man;
    I do not have human understanding.
3
I have not learned wisdom,
    nor have I attained to the knowledge of the Holy One.

4

Who has gone up to heaven and come down?
    Whose hands have gathered up the wind?
Who has wrapped up the waters in a cloak?
    Who has established all the ends of the earth?
What is his name, and what is the name of his son?
    Surely you know!

5

"Every word of God is flawless;
    he is a shield to those who take refuge in him.

6

Do not add to his words,
    or he will rebuke you and prove you a liar.

7

"Two things I ask of you, Lord;
    do not refuse me before I die:

8

Keep falsehood and lies far from me;
    give me neither poverty nor riches,
    but give me only my daily bread.

9

Otherwise, I may have too much and disown you
    and say, 'Who is the Lord?'
Or I may become poor and steal,
    and so dishonor the name of my God.

10

"Do not slander a servant to their master,
    or they will curse you, and you will pay for it.

11

"There are those who curse their fathers
    and do not bless their mothers;

12

those who are pure in their own eyes
    and yet are not cleansed of their filth;

13
those whose eyes are ever so haughty,
  whose glances are so disdainful;
14
those whose teeth are swords
  and whose jaws are set with knives
to devour the poor from the earth
  and the needy from among mankind.
15
"The leech has two daughters.
  'Give! Give!' they cry.
"There are three things that are never satisfied,
  four that never say, 'Enough!':
16
the grave, the barren womb,
  land, which is never satisfied with water,
  and fire, which never says, 'Enough!'
17
"The eye that mocks a father,
  that scorns an aged mother,
will be pecked out by the ravens of the valley,
  will be eaten by the vultures.
18
"There are three things that are too amazing for me,
  four that I do not understand:
19
the way of an eagle in the sky,
  the way of a snake on a rock,
the way of a ship on the high seas,
  and the way of a man with a young woman.
20
"This is the way of an adulterous woman:
  She eats and wipes her mouth
  and says, 'I've done nothing wrong.'

21

"Under three things the earth trembles,
    under four it cannot bear up:

22

a servant who becomes king,
    a godless fool who gets plenty to eat,

23

a contemptible woman who gets married,
    and a servant who displaces her mistress.

24

"Four things on earth are small,
    yet they are extremely wise:

25

Ants are creatures of little strength,
    yet they store up their food in the summer;

26

hyraxes are creatures of little power,
    yet they make their home in the crags;

27

locusts have no king,
    yet they advance together in ranks;

28

a lizard can be caught with the hand,
    yet it is found in kings' palaces.

29

"There are three things that are stately in their stride,
    four that move with stately bearing:

30

a lion, mighty among beasts,
    who retreats before nothing;

31

a strutting rooster, a he-goat,
    and a king secure against revolt.[b]

32

"If you play the fool and exalt yourself,
  or if you plan evil,
    clap your hand over your mouth!

33

For as churning cream produces butter,
  and as twisting the nose produces blood,
    so stirring up anger produces strife."

CHAPTER 31

Success

Repeat x 3: Gods plan for me is to be successful.

 One definition of success found in the Merriam Webster dictionary is a favorable or desired outcome. Measures of success will vary depending on the person you ask. It is said to be measured by your accomplishments. Although being a believer in Christ Jesus, spiritual success is be measured by the amount of people you bring to Christ through being his light here on earth. The Success I want to receive is a job well done by my Father in Heaven once my time hear on earth is up.

To reach success in whatever form financially or spiritually and accomplish your goals, 14 things you will need to do to help achieve your goals are 1. Love the Lord 1st before anything. He is the author of your story. 2. Love what you're trying to achieve, be passionate about it. 3. Get up and start your day early by working hard (the proof is in the PUT IN) and I do mean hard (you make an effort everyday to accomplishing the goal even when you don't feel like it). 4. Stay focused on the mission, keep a clear head. 5. Believe that the sky is the limit. 6. Serve others, meaning give to those less fortunate. 7. Create new ideas. 8. Remove all distractions and negative people. 9. Never stop pursuing your dream, don't give up until the mission is complete, be persistent. 10. Write down your goals. Keeping them in your head is just a dream. Put them on paper and they become a plan. 11. Create a realistic schedule that works for you and stick with it, be consistent. 12. Don't be afraid to leave things and people in the past who aren't apart of your mission. 13. Patience to endure the journey. Success takes time. 14. Fear not. Fear is not from God. So, remove any fear you may have, fear of the unknown, fear of failure and even fear of success yes, it is a real thing.

The Lord has placed these ideas inside of you, so he has already given you all that you need to be successful. Do not let the thoughts of "you aren't good enough" or "you don't have what it takes to pierce your heart." Your father in heaven would not place good thoughts within you to not provide all you need to have them fulfilled. All you have to do is believe. Have faith and put in the work.

A special characteristic that you will need to acquire along the way to be successful and the most important is prayer. This Journey is going to be a challenge just as everything else in life but stay focused because distractions will not stop just because you have a goal to reach. The devil, your enemy, will send more distractions your way to stop you from reaching your goal. FOCUS means removing people, devices, social media, anything that will be a hindrance to you reaching your goal. The enemy will bring people from the past that you thought you got rid of, he will magically have people DM (direct message) you, whatever your weakness, he knows it and he will target it, over and over. His goal is to keep you stagnant so notice them when they come and try your hardest to avoid the distractions at all cost. Constant prayer is needed. I believe in you!

Reinforce this habit, once you are committed to something, make the decision, and dedicate your all to achieving it. If you want to play basketball, practice all the time, practice makes perfect, if you want to dance, sing, or start a business, stick to it, and keep your word to yourself. To accomplish anything you put your mind to, you will need to do what you have to do even when you don't feel like doing it. Just do it anyway. Perseverance goes hand and hand with commitment. Commitment is the decision and perseverance is the action.

Your dream may take years to achieve, be patient, this will not be an overnight process. It will not happen if you do not make it happen. Don't think just because you have been at this for 3 years you should have already been successful by now so you might as well give up. Just think: if Madame CJ Walker would have given up when no one wanted to purchase her hair cream, she would not be spoken about in the history books. What if Tyler Perry would have stopped pursuing his dream after being turned down by many producers and becoming homeless. Never give up on yourself. You have to really believe you can do all things through Him who gives you strength. Philippians 4:13 (NIV)

God wants you to dream big because he is a Big God. He knows you couldn't have done it on your own, so he has your back. Be obedient and complete the mission, then you will have to give him all the praise and say "It was no one, but you God. Thank You, Lord." Everything you need is right on the other side of fear. The Bible commands you not to be afraid for the Lord your God is with you. There is no limit with Christ. So, let's not become weary of doing what is good. For at the proper time, we will reap a harvest if we don't give up. Galatians 6:9 New International Version.

The events your life are actually summed up in this one quote that continues to motivate and helps me through my-not-so-good days: It says "Eventually all the pieces fall into place, until then laugh at confusion, live for the moment and believe that everything happens for a reason." - unknown

Prayer: Thank you, Lord, for the dreams you have placed inside of me. Help me to discipline myself so that I may fulfill everything you have planned for me. Remove any fear and anxiety so I can be prosperous in your call for my life. I give you all the honor and praise in your mighty name, Amen.

Proverbs 31

Sayings of King Lemuel

1

The sayings of King Lemuel—an inspired utterance his mother taught him.

2

Listen, my son! Listen, son of my womb!
  Listen, my son, the answer to my prayers!

3

Do not spend your strength[a] on women,
  your vigor on those who ruin kings.

4

It is not for kings, Lemuel—Sa
  it is not for kings to drink wine,
  not for rulers to crave beer,

5

lest they drink and forget what has been decreed,
  and deprive all the oppressed of their rights.

6

Let beer be for those who are perishing,
  wine for those who are in anguish!

7

Let them drink and forget their poverty
  and remember their misery no more.

8

Speak up for those who cannot speak for themselves,
  for the rights of all who are destitute.

9

Speak up and judge fairly;
  defend the rights of the poor and needy.

Epilogue: The Wife of Noble Character

10

[b]A wife of noble character who can find?
  She is worth far more than rubies.

11
Her husband has full confidence in her
   and lacks nothing of value.
12
She brings him good, not harm,
   all the days of her life.
13
She selects wool and flax
   and works with eager hands.
14
She is like the merchant ships,
   bringing her food from afar.
15
She gets up while it is still night;
   she provides food for her family
   and portions for her female servants.
16
She considers a field and buys it;
   out of her earnings she plants a vineyard.
17
She sets about her work vigorously;
   her arms are strong for her tasks.
18
She sees that her trading is profitable,
   and her lamp does not go out at night.
19
In her hand she holds the distaff
   and grasps the spindle with her fingers.
20
She opens her arms to the poor
   and extends her hands to the needy.
21
When it snows, she has no fear for her household;
   for all of them are clothed in scarlet.

22

She makes coverings for her bed;
    she is clothed in fine linen and purple.

23

Her husband is respected at the city gate,
    where he takes his seat among the elders of the land.

24

She makes linen garments and sells them,
    and supplies the merchants with sashes.

25

She is clothed with strength and dignity;
    she can laugh at the days to come.

26

She speaks with wisdom,
    and faithful instruction is on her tongue.

27

She watches over the affairs of her household
    and does not eat the bread of idleness.

28

Her children arise and call her blessed;
    her husband also, and he praises her:

29

"Many women do noble things,
    but you surpass them all."

30

Charm is deceptive, and beauty is fleeting;
    but a woman who fears the Lord is to be praised.

31

Honor her for all that her hands have done,
    and let her works bring her praise at the city gate.

CONCLUSION

Hey Baby Girl, I ask that once you read this book and let it sink in just a little. To receive all the information and for all of it to make sense, read it 2 more times. It's beneficial. I can only help you by telling you what has helped me and what has guided me along the way. It's up to you to take the advice. I'm nowhere near perfect by far but I am chasing after the Lord, praising His name with every move I make and in return He has His arms around me guiding me every day.

Just ask God for what you need, and He provides. He will show you what you need to see and keep you away from what you don't need to see. Our father in Heaven knows each of our needs. He will make sure you have what you need when you need it. Humility is needed in order to allow the lord to fully be in control. So, in the meantime, have faith while you sit back and allow God to direct your path, while eating a piece of humble pie, knowing that he has your best interest at heart. Jesus loves you. Trust in the Lord that He has your back, and He will never let you down. He might not show up when you want Him to, but He will show up right on time.

When I say trust in the Lord, what I mean is you have to really trust him, completely. Trust his timing for things to happen in your life. Trust and believe that He will not leave you to handle things on your own, but that He will always come through. No matter how hard the situation may seem. Prayer is the answer. The title of this book helped me through the hardest times of my life. When God answers your prayers, you will feel this amazing unexplainable feeling. Like a hug from God. I would like to think you get tingly feelings knowing you are loved. If you don't believe me, try it for yourself. That's the only way to believe: experience it for yourself. As you go through life always stay true to your word and stay focused on the Lord. He will make your crooked paths straight.

Prayer: Thank you, Father for loving me. I will not let fear, evil thoughts, hurt, betrayal, doubt, or uncertainty of your love for me. I will not let those things enter my heart to deviate from your plans for me. You are so amazing, Lord. I am so grateful to be a part of your creations. I am nothing without you. But I can accomplish all things with you. I will trust you always. Thank you for bringing me where I'm from to where I am today. As a result of your grace and mercy. I am Blessed and highly favored, I am the head and not the tail, I am above and not beneath. I know through it all I will survive. Detach the things that hinder me from my purpose. I give you total control over my life. I will trust in you, Lord. As long as I have breath to praise you Lord, Jesus I will. All of my praises belong to you Lord. You have held me and kept me. Your greatness is so wonderful, I will forever be grateful. You are the King of Glory. I honor you, Lord. You are so worthy to be praised. Thank You, Lord. Thank You, Lord. Thank You, Lord. I love you Father, Amen.

Printed in the United States
by Baker & Taylor Publisher Services